AQUARIUS HOROSCOPE 2023

Your essential guide to love, money, happiness and using moon magic!

Hi guys,

A warm welcome to all my regular readers and a special hello to all new readers. I aim to provide a comprehensive insight into 2023 with spiritual, psychological insight, and down to earth common sense advice.

Every year when I write these books I just cannot believe how fast the year has gone, and that it's once again time to write and publish the series for the next year.

As many of you know, I've been producing these books since 2014, and boy has the world changed since then and 2023 will be a year of unprecedented change in world terms, that's why I've decided to also do an Astrology book of World predictions which include predictions for countries and certain leaders, because I feel that we need to be forwarded and for armed.

It's important to remember that no matter what is happening in the outside world, we all have our lives to live and karma to resolve and we must enjoy our own unique journey. Remember, we are all meant to be here at this very time, to experience what we are experiencing and we should never underestimate our own power and ability to thrive and make a difference.

Yes, we are all at different points along our own personal journey, but what I want to do with these books is encourage you all to understand your own creativity, power and never to underestimate yourself, to feel lost all to lose a sense of purpose. We are all here for a reason and we all have a valuable contribution to make in different ways, and hopefully my annual books have inspired you to understand your purpose and connect with some inspiration.

Fortunately the Saturn Square Uranus that was happening between
Saturn in Aquarius and Uranus in Taurus is now done and dusted,
which is a good thing because that was creating an enormous amount
of tension within all of us, because the energies of Saturn and
Uranus are so different. However, what we have coming this year is
Pluto moving into Aquarius, and every time Pluto has changed signs
there have been dramatic events worldwide that have changed
history: it could be the birth of new countries, technological changes,
conflict, economic shifts, innovations and the advent of new
philosophies or political systems. So we should all be ready to
embrace change with an open mind and we should remember not to
be overly concerned with things that we are not able to change,
because what we all can change is our attitude and it's always better
to be optimistic and proactive.

I've often seen in my career as an astrologer that astrology works
best for people who make plans, who act on those plans, who
motivate themselves and who don't wait around for things to happen.
Good things happen when we take chances, when we get up and
seize opportunities or even just envisage then, very little happens we
stick to comfort zones, resist change and hang onto the past for dear
life, irrespective of the planets.

I always believe that it's important to understand our roots, to know
where we come from and how our experiences have shaped us and
given us wisdom. Our cumulative heritage is always important, but
we can't live in the past, things are changing and we have to keep
moving along and adapting, and using our wits and innate dynamic
energy to thrive.

Love Lisa

AQUARIUS HOROSCOPE 2023 – What's in store?

This is actually a highly significant year for Aquarius because the power planet Pluto is about to move into Aquarius for the first time in over 240 years.

Now while Pluto will be in Aquarius for a number of decades, the movement of Pluto into Aquarius next year marks the start of a radical new phase of development for you. Next year, particularly around April, is an excellent time for you to start reassessing your life and doing a big life audit. This is an opportunity for you to think about everything you've ever wanted to do, your ambitions, your aspirations and also your spiritual goals and understand what you need to do going forward.

This is a fantastic year for making radical decisions, for purging yourself of past toxic relationships or activities, for turning over a new leaf and also for having a whole new mindset. Pluto is the planet of psychology, so it's not just about manifestations in the outer world, it's about going deep into the core of your being and understanding yourself. So it's all about developing greater self-awareness, understanding your potential and your power, and then realizing what the blockages are, both within your own thought patterns and within the outside world, and then creatively moving forward with determination to overcome those obstacles.

So a brand new life is available to you, it all depends how much you are prepared to work on yourself and to weed out any regressive thinking. It's all about change and accepting the new, however the choice is down to you, if you are happy where you are, there's no need for you to do anything and you may not feel the impetus, but this would be a lost opportunity for growth.

With Jupiter being in Aries from the beginning of the year, this should supercharge your positive thinking. You tend to be more likely to feel buoyant and upbeat and you should feel more supported by you everyday environment. So while your own attitude picks up and becomes more optimistic, you will also find you're interacting with more people who have a good attitude to life, are proactive and have a positive spirit, and this will further reinforce your optimism about the year ahead.

With Jupiter going into Taurus later in the year, this is also a fantastic time for healing within the family arena, improving family relationships and for re-establishing bonds with your nearest and dearest.

Aquarius tend to have a very private side, very often they thrive in an environment where they are free to think, where they get away from it all, either in nature or in a secluded environment so they can contemplate and pontificate, and this is a very important year for you to do that. So while family is incredibly important and there may be some big and significant family events, you also must have you time and space by yourself to undergo all these important thought processes, some dredging up and some reassessing of the past, with the idea of putting a more positive gloss on it.

Excited and expanded thinking

The first half of the year is an excellent time for you work life, this is a fantastic time for you to do some learning, to improve your skills and these could include language skills, computer languages or just understanding technology better. You rather enjoy learning and so if you have decided your life is in a rut, it's ideal for you to sign up for some courses, particularly if these involve little bit of travel and a brand new subject matter.

Ready for mind mingling

The year is off to a very busy start and yet it should be quite interesting, there's an opportunity to mingle with people that are different to what you have experienced before. You might be doing this mingling because you have new colleagues, you're in a slightly different job, or because you're doing this extra study which is opening in your mind and bringing you into contact with more vibrant people.

Writing you way to success

The first part of the year is wonderful for all your social media marketing and also communications goals, so if you need to work on improving your website and jazzing up you resumes or just improving the way you interact with your client and consumer base, you should do that. It's also a great time for any journalistic work, whether you are actually writing for a living or just enjoy being active in social media publishing or blogging. This is an excellent time for expressing opinions and gaining quite a following.

You can be quite a prolific writer and so whatever you're writing about, you're going to be generating a lot of it.

Day tripping

Short distance travel is much more a feature of the start of the year and you may travel because of work, to do training or selling, but it's also important for you and you partner to have short city breaks and romantic getaways on the weekend. So it's not only a time of working hard but playing hard, and even if you can't afford to necessarily go on a holiday to a different city, you and you partner should definitely use the weekends to do things you've never done before, to interact with different sorts of people and get yourselves some exciting challenges which will make weekends a bit of an adventure.

Cyber relationships

Internet dating and long distance relationships can be quite successful this year, because you find it very easy to express yourself in writing. Relationships that are mainly based around messaging and an electronic relationship are very fulfilling for you. You're definitely looking for a partner who is open minded and inspirational, because this year you want to think big and you want to think a lot about the future and the possibilities, and thus you need a partner who is going to open up you horizons, rather than dragging you into a very safe and stuffy place.

Your inner Indiana Jones

The free-spirited, adventurer side of Aquarius is definitely awakened in the first part of the year, and this is the time when you're going to be most expressive and expansive, and probably a little bit erratic too. Sometimes you bite off more than you can chew and you can engage in risky behavior because you just feel like taking a chance on things, but on the other hand it's a great way to suddenly open up new opportunities just by doing things that are out of character, or slightly more riske that you normally would.

Family values

In the second half of the year, with Jupiter in Taurus and also retrograde in Taurus for a period, there is definitely an opportunity for reflection. This is when you should do your life audit. You really need to get to grips with everything that's going on at surface, and also a deeper level, so this is an excellent time to think about things that happened in the recent or distant past, and develop more positive opinions about the lessons you're learnt, rather than the regret, pain or finger pointing.

This is a very important year for forgiveness, you need to forgive yourself and others and you should certainly work hard at healing within the family circle. So if there are any family members whom you've fallen out with, or have had bad relations with, this is an excellent time to restore the relationship, or even if that's not possible, to at least issue apologies and absolve each other of the guilt and the angst.

Your home is you castle

This is an excellent time for you to start thinking about redecorating you home, or any home improvements. It's also a good time for house hunting and looking for real estate, so if you and your family want to move, be it locally or internationally, this is a great time to be seeking a new home. Alternatively, because family life and home life is very important to your sense of belonging and security, it's time to make the home environment more livable, and you guys may want to make improvements that mean it's easier to entertain, or where all the family members are better accommodated and happy.

You're definitely more keen on entertaining but sometimes you leave yourself depleted because you can bite off more than you can chew.

Reunions

This could be a time of family reunions where you travels, or have family to stay that you haven't seen in a very, very long time. There may be big family events like weddings, anniversaries, big birthdays etc. so all in all family will be more important, and the focus will fall on family relationships which will come under the spotlight.

This is definitely an opportunity for you to draw strength from your roots, from your family values and to recognize again where you have come from, where you have been and what is most important in your life.

Work opportunities

This year there are lots of opportunities for Aquarius who work in research, particularly to do with the environment and ecology, there may also be excellent job opportunities in these fields. It's also a good year for Aquarius who work in real estate, culture, tourism and hospitality.

Romance is red hot

During the first 3 months of the year Mars is in Gemini which represents you solar fifth house, and this brings a huge amount of energy to the dating sphere. So you will begin to feel quite amorous and romantic during the first part of the year, thus it's excellent for date nights with a partner, and for injecting a little bit of spontaneity and some surprises into the relationship. So it's very important in the first few months not to be passive in ongoing relationships, it's time for you to be assertive in establishing some new directions and some challenges for you and your partner, and for encouraging you both to be more active socially and just to learn to enjoy life again.

Your inner impetuous child is definitely activated in the first few months, you can be rather impatient, restless and quite mischievous. You're inclined to joke around, play pranks and you always want to indulge you eccentricities. So this being said, you can actually create a lot of excitement in relationships, but if you energy is a little bit out of sync with your partner's energy, you could actually be seen as a little bit aggressive or reckless.

Child's play

The first part of the year is excellent for you engaging with children, so it's great for important discussions with your children, for showing them leadership and maybe for being more hands-on in helping children with their development as far as learning, psychological or creative goes. You may find your children challenge you more and possibly take up more of your time, but a lot of respect can grow because you begin to interact with you children in a different way, but it's important for you to be the adult and to show your alpha characteristics to imbue your children with a lot of strength and courage.

Competitive spirit

January to March is excellent for very competitive activities, so whether you need to excel on a sporting field or just show what you're made of in terms of management decisions or leadership, this is a good time to go for it.

If there's something that you are concerned about and which needs to be tackled, the sooner in the year you tackle it, the better, because you optimism, courage and ability to make a difference is energized in this period. You can access you power potential to the greatest extent in the first few months.

The year unfolds

While Aquarius are pretty confident and optimistic throughout the year, the energy later in the year is a little bit more about understanding, knowledge, curiosity, assimilation etc. whereas at the beginning of the year, it's more about getting things done, breaking down barriers and responding assertively to challenges.

Relationship dynamics

Venus is retrograde in Leo during the height of the summer months in the Northern Hemisphere, and Leo represents your solar seventh house, so this is a very important time for emotional development in relationships.

On one hand, this is a time where you can be more affectionate and where you and you partner can be more cooperative. Teamwork improves and you can have productive discussions, however it's not just about what's going on at the surface, it is also an opportunity for you and you partner to develop a more significant understanding.

If you are married and you and you partner are generally getting on well, but there is a lack of fundamental compatibility, or one of both of you feel unfulfilled by the relationship, then this can be glaringly obvious in the summer months, and one or both of you may feel lonely or frustrated, and the frustration can be sexual or emotional.

This is an ideal time for you and your partner to reassess how well you're really connecting, whether you are able to nurture each other and to truly work together as a couple, or whether you both just pay lip service to these things and you just go along to get along.

Good relationships where there was a lot of chemistry and a great deal of love, should be worked hard upon to restore trust, quality communication and affection.

In struggling relationships, this is a time to acknowledge what went wrong, when it went wrong, if it can be fixed and how to fix it. This is not a time for you guys to be ostriches and deny any underlying unhappiness in the relationship, it's definitely a time to get to grips with things, to fix things and to have those difficult to have meaningful conversations.

The Crunch

What the summer months should prove to Aquarius and your partner, is how willing or not both of you are to adapt, to seriously re-engage with each other and to bring the spark alive, because sometimes couples are quite happy to just drift along and suffer in silence because they either don't believe the relationship can get better, or have basically given up. However, I think it's both very important for Aquarius to inject faith and optimism into the relationship, and to show you commitment and faith that the relationship can and will get better, and then for you both to take a more positive approach, and take steps forward to turn over new leaves whenever possible.

Being a cool headed mover and shaker

Along with common sense, it is important for you to be self-disciplined and to apply focus, this is not a good year for you to go forward with a hazard approach. Although you try a lot of things and the first half of the year can be more experimental and a little bit haphazard, as the year goes on you must knuckle down on and achieve that focus.

This year is certainly a case of what doesn't kill you makes you stronger, but at the same time you shouldn't face any particularly big challenges in the outside world as such, the challenges you face are more within your own mindset.

Standing tall

This year it's important for you to remember who you are and you must dig deep, and if you do this with a true sense of purpose and identity, you can have victory and you can overcome problems with confidence and control.

The key to your success this year is in you being grounded, pragmatic and using your common sense and then applying these factors to any situation will stand your in good stead.

You're a stalwart

Aquarius can be stubborn and this year your stubbornness is much needed, as you will have to apply willpower to overcoming obstacles and dealing with adversity.

Doing it all again

It's very important for you to draw on past experience, so in every situation you must understand how it is similar to previous situations, and if you have been successful in these situations before you should be successful again. However, you should be quick to recognize situations that are a potential repeat of previous of failures and now it is your opportunity to redo them, but differently and thus to have a successful outcome.

People are always asked whether if they had their life to live again they would live it differently and almost everyone says that they would like to tweak a few things. What people don't realize is that while we can't start our lives again from scratch, every day is a new opportunity to do things differently, but if we haven't learn from our mistakes and achieved some wisdom as we go through life that can be difficult to do. So the challenge for Aquarius this year, is to be able to understand the lessons of the past and apply them to the future to ensure that mistakes are corrected, and situations, where in the past you have failed, now become successful.

So as you can tell this is a year when you have a chance to change the record, wipe the slate clean and set a slightly different agenda through changing your psychology, your thinking or the kind of energy you enter into situations with.

Gaining the advantage

Sometimes you can gain by playing your opponent's off against each other, and this is why timing and patience is very important to you. This year it's not just about surging ahead regardless, it's about waiting for your opportunity and striking while the time is right and making your move strategically.

This year the best way to go about your goals is with determination and patience, but also in a non-linear way. So it's the case of 3 steps forward, two steps back but you are still moving forward and that's what counts.

Last one standing

There is a strong need that you have to prevail and have the last word, you don't necessarily have to win but it's more about out lasting the competition in a war of attrition. So while you may not be the fastest out the blocks, what's important this year is staying power and making sure that you're there at the end to cross the line and this is what you should strive for.

You should never forget that in striving for you goal, you are learning important lessons and understanding more about yourself, as well as having the opportunity to correct past mistakes. So it's the journey that counts rather than the actual goal itself which could actually be secondary.

The sun is rising and possibilities abound

You may go into this year not knowing what you focus or you goals are even going to be, in some cases you might suddenly embark on a plan or project simply because of an outside challenge, or because you are presented with a dilemma which means that you must find a solution which in turn means you stumble upon a new path. So often fate helps nudge you in the right direction from the start of 2023.

Looking after #1

It's important for you to look after yourself and your needs, this is an important year for you to get to grips with what makes you secure and brings satisfaction and fulfilment to you life. It's a time where you need to clear away the clutter of superficial and frivolous activities and get down to the basics that actually most valuable to you in life.

In relationships you must be more confident about expressing your desires, being affectionate and amorous and you should be more vocal about what you crave in an intimate relationship. You need to develop more faith in yourself and to fundamentally know who you are and what you stand for, and the more you can define this, the easier it is for you to express yourself emotionally, and this helps relationships become more harmonious and more authentic.

Taming you wild side

It's important for you to channel you more aggressive nature, sometimes you express aggression by being a little bit controversial, stirring the pot or getting other people wound up while you stays calm, but you need to own you own aggression and express it in ways that are more constructive. Often the best way for you to express your aggressive energy is by driving, writing letters, taking spontaneous short trips, getting stuck into physically demanding home improvement projects, clearing out the attic or renovating/restoring something.

Uncontrollable, unaddressed aggression can be very destructive and can lead to physical illness, but if you're able to harness it by using a proactive, positive approach to improving you private life or family life, your overall well-being will increase.

It's time to be king of you castle, that doesn't just mean that you must enjoy being the patriarch/matriach in terms of the family, it also means that you must be the master of your emotions, you impulses and your anger. You must be the boss in terms of controlling yourself and projecting positive power to bring security to you family.

Essence and Energies – "First when there's nothing
But a slow glowing dream
That your fear seems to hide
Deep inside your mind"

The essence in the first month of the year is decisions and making the break. This is an excellent time for taking important decisions, especially when it involves moving on and putting something in the past. So it's time to turn your back on something, it could be some activity, an association with a person or group or a bad habit, but it's time to draw a line and move on.

Making decisions is a way of grabbing power, procrastination, putting things off and delaying are ways in which our power ebbs away from us, and we end up feeling less powerful and more victims of fate. So the theme this year is for Aquarius to gain back the initiative in your life and you can start from the very first month of the year by taking decisions, stepping up to the plate, biting the bullet and saying this is how I intend to go on.

Sometimes this month you have to be quite ruthless, so don't worry about being abrupt in the way that you end an activity or association. Time is of the essence and there's no point in spending more energy or time flogging dead horses, so free up your energy for exciting phases of renewal in your life.

Affirmation: "I strive for creative change and renewal in my life and I know that power comes to me when I'm decisive."

Love and Romance

In terms of dating, you may draw disruptive people into your life, who may criticize you, question you or perhaps they excite you, because they arouse something in you that was missing or dormant and that can be a little bit disconcerting.

Emotions in new relationships tend to run deep, and this is a very passionate time in your life when you care a great deal about the deeper aspects of a new relationship or the more private and secretive side of your partner.

You have the ability right now to transform you attitudes and mindsets about dating and thus transform the path of future relationships, increasing their success rate and the sense of fulfillment within them.

While a new relationship could begin this month, the relationship may not be successful if you have not properly cut ties and resolved a previous relationship. This is not a good time for rebound relationships, you need to make sure that you have totally settled the feelings connected to a previous partnership, ensuring that you're not still hankering over that partnership.

It's highly likely that a relationship that begins now will have a certain element of fatefulness attached, or even a possible past life connection, which could mean that the relationship gets deep very quickly, but it could also mean that there's some hidden complications that will really challenge you, but which could be very important in terms of your psychological and spiritual growth this year.

Career and Aspiration

You are inclined to be secretive and play your cards close to your chest this month. You will draw up plans in secret and hold out on full disclosure. You need to be careful that you don't hold back information which can later be tracked back to a specific date and thus bring you judgment in sitting on it into question. Sometimes you get to find out something, and you hold back on letting others know to either gain an advantage or protect someone's feelings; however, once you do release the information, it often comes to light that you knew all along, and even if you had the best intentions, you could have some explaining to do.

There is quite a bit of tension this month, and you are taking life seriously; it is not a time of taking things with a pinch of salt. You will take decisions seriously and will dwell over the facts for many days before reaching a conclusion.

Venus is a planet associated with pleasure, good times, partying and great feelings of affection, and it's certainly possible to increase the amount of loving interaction with your partner. However, there is a more serious side to Venus as it is associated with debate, negotiation and coming to compromises. Thus it's quite important in all aspects of your life to be working hard, at your business and interpersonal relationships, to get more out of them and that includes working on cooperation, teamwork and sometimes being a little bit more conciliatory.

Adventure and Motivation

More is more in January – more work and more play, you are having a full schedule of activity. This is a very social time when you are mixing with a variety of social groups and new business associates. Even though you are highly industrious, dedicated to work and willing to work long hours, you will not compromise on fun, especially when it involves going out with you partner.

This may be a very spiritually rewarding time if you have a religion or a faith. You tend to be drawn to spiritual concepts and you're more likely to reflect and take stock of your life in a philosophical way.

This month is excellent for you to enjoy and succeed in you artistic and creative goals. You are highly inspired and feel guided to produce emotionally provocative works of art.

This is an excellent time for sailing, traveling and going on retreats.

Your intuition provides insight and dreams may be precognitive. You may experience hunches and even visions, déjà vu or sudden flashes of insight.

Marriage and Family

This is a month of rather strange and disconcerting emotions in love relationships. You or your partner may be quite moody, you may have periods where you guys feel a little bit sullen and withdrawn, and you may have other periods when you feel particularly passionate about things. In marriage, moods can fluctuate more wildly and sometimes they even confuse you both. It's hard to get clarity and transparency, however although answers are hard to come by, if you guys are observant and emotionally intelligent, a lot can be gleamed about what really goes on at a subtle level in relationships.

This is a time when you and a partner have to deal with endings, you may have to finish a relationship or separate from a partner. Alternatively you and you partner may have to enter a purging and consolidation phase where you guys end a contract, association or an activity and then there is a period of relief or possibly grieving in connection with this, but it is a time of cutting your losses and moving on.

During this month, karma is a very important factor in love. Things from the past will have a large effect on this current month in terms of the events and outcomes, so in order to successfully navigate your relationships, it may be important to go over old ground, to resolve differences and clear up any misunderstandings.

Success in a relationship right now is being honest with yourself about feelings of anger, resentment or hurt that you are harboring and unable to let go off, and also to examine whether your partner is maybe carrying around some similar feelings right now. The relationship will continue to stumble along unless a concerted effort to address these lingering problems is made as they are the secret enemies in your relationship.

Money and Finance

This month the whole is often worth more than the sum of the parts and the difference is you and your ability to get the best out of people and motivate and enthuse, or maybe apply pressure to improve their service to you .

This month is about squeezing out more from the assets, services or products you already use. Often it's about new creative uses of resources to save money.

Enhance love magic

This is not a time when Aquarius can survive in a restrictive or controlling relationship. You can be quite argumentative – however, in happy, positive relationships you can be funny and inspiring; it is only where there are deeper issues that you will be inclined to be perverse and confrontational.

In terms of love magic, this month is wonderful for long distance relationships, alternate relationships and open relationships as it favors progressive thinking in love. Couples who are travelling together, especially on tours which are very adventurous or even bohemian or spiritually inspired can establish a renewed connection. You should be more patient in love and to try and explain yourself better to prevent confusion as you may not realize how mixed the signals you are sending are.

Planetary Cautions

Rest is important this month, and your digestion can suffer due to worry and stress. You are inclined to be pessimistic, which is not like you at all, and so you should not take these cautious and often pessimistic thoughts too seriously; it is a phase.

This is an excellent month for in-depth work involving technical detail – you can concentrate and knuckle down to grind through work that at other times you would find highly laborious. However it's less good for public debate or high pressure public occasions where you feel exposed and put on the spot.

You will be very pleased with what you achieve by month end, even if you do have quite a few moans and grumbles as you go along.

*Essence and Energies – **"I must be looking for something
Something sacred I lost
But the river is wide
And it's too hard to cross"***

This month has two elements, there's the private you vs the public you. In public you can show a lot of confidence, this is an excellent time to be assertive, to take leadership and control of your life and even to make your mark on the world by doing something that will bring you a lot of recognition.

However, although the public side of you is quite forceful and confident, the private side of you is very insecure and unsure right now. So you'll have to turn your attention inward and focus strongly on your feelings and what is going on inside of yourself. You are quite easily triggered and can be quite sensitive right now, and it's often important to get the root of these feelings. You should use the feelings that come about when you interact with people as an important pointer to whatever is going on inside of yourself, because while your external life can be quite successful, there is still quite a lot of work to do internally right now

If you pay attention, it will be easy to identify where your vulnerabilities are and you can use that to make sure that you go ahead on your own terms, rather than on someone else's. A particular 'thing' to look out for right now, is excessive people pleasing, because that can often be a sign of insecurity that needs to be addressed.

Affirmation: "I resolve to be totally honest with myself and that's the key to internal resolution and happiness."

Love and Romance

Aquarius who have been attracting partners who are very different, as that has been seen as exciting and daring, will find those relationships are now having teething problems as there is perhaps no common ground to create a fabric to hold the relationship together. However, with an open mind and some hard work, this can be resolved.

During this month relationships can be hard work but you shouldn't be discouraged, as often the effort you put in to show commitment, be a good listener and improve understanding yields dividends. So while things in both love and relationships moves very slowly and often with annoyance, if you're patient and consistent and put in effort to achieve balance, harmony and fairness in your relationship, then you will certainly see dividends.

This may be a month of very important decisions and dilemmas in love, you may feel that you are at a crossroads and are weighing up important options. It's very important not to rush into anything, you should go about things slowly, methodically and take all the details into account.

What's important this month, is to stick to the facts. It's very easy to become distracted by feelings of doubt or insecurity in love, so it's very important to be clear on what is real and what is not, because the last thing you want to do is to upset yourself about something imagined. This is certainly a time where your imagination can run away from you, especially if you're feeling vulnerable or a little bit overtired. So sometimes just managing your stress levels, the amount of sleep you're getting and your diet can actually lead to better relationships because you are more likely to be in a calm, rational frame of mind.

The biggest threat in love right now is getting things out of proportion or misinterpreting. So it's always wise to straighten things out, to prevent misunderstandings and be clear on what is actually being said rather than what you have interpreted. So again, use your logic and rationale, rely on facts and don't let negative feelings turn into a self-fulfilling prophecy of doom and gloom in relationships.

Career and Aspiration

This month you will work hard and will not suffer fools or the lazy gladly. You have have business acumen, determination and drive a hard bargain. Although you're wise and cautious with money, sometimes caution is a stumbling block for you and the odd burst of impulsive action plays to your advantage and stops you getting into a rut.

Frustration at obstacles is part of this month and the patience and persistence or indeed stubbornness which is part of you Aquarius nature will have to be called upon – but it is not just about being patient is it about using that waiting time and those passing storms to prepare better, analyses you maps and to get that boat into perfect nick before you're able to set sail once again.

This is an excellent time for all those of you who are spokespeople and who are particularly interested in the charitable or humanitarian sphere. This is also an ideal time for those careers that involve subjects that are slightly more esoteric and less well defined, so these could be subjects to do with the art world, politics or philosophy, and Aquarius who write on or research in these areas can be particularly inspired.

Adventure and Motivation

This month asks you the question; how hard are you prepared to work for what you want, and how tenacious are you in pursuing goals? If you're not willing to back up your ideas with detailed plans, consistent effort and willingness to go back to the drawing board, adjust and regroup, then maybe you do not want it badly enough.

Your ideas and beliefs will be challenged and tested – you will find that others think your truth is invalid and you should get ready to fight you corner and show how much you really do believe what you do. But you should not let anyone censor you – you have a right to your beliefs. You need to make sure your words and deeds are aligned this month, or you may be accused of hypocrisy or double standards, but following this advice will lead to adventure as this is you connecting with your true Aquarius spirit.

Marriage and Family

If you're been with a partner for many years, it's time to finally tie the knot, especially if you do it on a trip away spontaneously.

Spiritual values matter to you in relationships, and those marriages which are founded on strong moral or religious values will thrive and can weather storms with love getting stronger. This is a tougher month for those relationships in which you both come from different religions or where one has a very different moral code. In these mixed religion/mixed value relationships, you guys will have to work harder to find common ground, especially in connection with bringing up the children, which can be a big bone of contention.

You may need to help out a sibling, but you may need to exhibit some tough love – it is not about only offering help and sympathy, it is about being a wise and restraining influence. In some cases, you may decide that distancing yourself from a sibling is the only way to get them to own up to a problem.

In fact getting back to basics, being really simplistic and learning to appreciate the most fundamental things in your life that make you happy, is important. This is not the time to chase after pie in the sky, to long for what you don't have or to become obsessed with airy fairy ideals. It's a time to be pragmatic, to be grounded and to draw strength from all the positives in your life rather than wasting energy chasing after rainbows in the sky.

Family and home life are very important. However, other than spending time with family in a relaxed environment, it's also a wonderful time for perhaps buying pieces of art, decorating or doing things to make your home feel more special, more comforting and more like a place where you can take refuge from the world.

Money and Finance

Decisions this month are more difficult as they tend to be complex, multi-faceted and will affect not only you but others you care about. Choices made often exhibit a trade-off between short-term and longer terms goals, and so you have to be very clear about the longer term impact of what you decide.

You should be really careful about investing and spending. It's important to listen to your instincts and use emotional intelligence when dealing with business associates.

This is a very good month for work involving charity, art and music.

Living and Loving to the Full

This month the way to enhance life is a little unusual but also profound, often to bring beauty into a relationship, you have to bring more beauty into you life, alone or with a partner. So deepening you relationship to beauty whether it's as an artist or by supporting and appreciating other artists or paying greater attention to the exquisite perfection and symmetry in nature, can rewire you attention to what

is subtle, unique and beautiful in terms of the enduring qualities that
emerge within you love relationship or romance.

You can then be more receptive to the synchronicity that underlies
you existence, as patterns in love often become more recognizable.
Understanding how certain elements of your love life fit together can
bring you peace and greater relationship harmony and satisfaction.
You must allow yourself to see and feel without judgment so that
you can glimpse the beauty in the symphony of you life.

Planetary Cautions

This is a time when things are very confusing, nothing is black and
white and it's hard to find answers. You may be inclined to tell white
lies and others may be less than transparent with you, and so you
have to make sure what the facts really are. This is why you mustn't
be too dogmatic or gung ho.

This may not be a good time for financial negotiations as there are
too many unknowns and too much ambivalence among the parties.

This is not a great time for legal and financial dealings or analysis.
It's good to stay flexible and keep an open mind.

Emotions can cloud judgment especially if you're already in an upset
or confused frame of mind, so you shouldn't take important decisions
when emotional.

Moon Magic

The new moon phase extends from the 20th of February to the 7th of
March, this waxing phase is the perfect fortnight for new initiatives,
setting plans, establishing goals, starting anything prospective and

being proactive. This is the action phase, details below:

The waxing phase is excellent for brand new starts in fields where you have no experience. Competitive and physically demanding tasks are favored. Getting treatments like physiotherapy, osteotherapy, chiropractic therapy or reflexology is successful. A good time to meet new people and present yourself favorably. Careers needing confidence and assertiveness are favored.

A good waxing phase for negotiation and deal making. Excellent for important discussions in relationships and making decisions. Great for IT, marketing and social media projects. Journalism and writing is successful. A good time for planning, brainstorming and gathering information. You should prepare carefully for interviews or public discussion. A good time to plan trips for business and pleasure.

A successful time for dating and forming new romantic opportunities. This favors new business ventures in entertainment and leisure. Creative and artistic ventures are successful. It's suitable for competitive sports and other pursuit involving confidence and fire. Going out to concerts and events is favored. Good for business involving children and young people.

Essence and Energies – "Running with the night."

This month it's important to go where the energy leads you, and you should go with the flow, feeling your way along rather than assuming that you already know the answers, because guess what? You are in for a surprise.

Being mindful and totally open to messages from the universe is an essential ingredient for getting the most out of this month; this means being alert and aware without making any pre-judgments. You should then respond to whatever the situation presents in a spontaneous and timely way. March is typically a time to adopt a reactive mode, following the cues that life presents with an attitude of experimenting and learning.

What can make this period challenging for Aquarius is that you are more sensitive and emotional which can bring about unexpected moods which leave you feeling a little confused or even annoyed with yourself. However, this month is actually key to understanding your lesser acknowledged emotions and learning to bring them to the surface and to appreciate where they come from and the role they play.

The lesson is to understand that living in the moment can require action, turning away, or even saying NO. Going with the flow is not the same as being passive, it's simply aligning your energy with the universe and learning to understand what's not necessarily logical, but what makes sense on an emotional level.

This is an important time to understand the subtle ways in which your life is slowly changing, it is important to realize that no situation lasts forever, and that things will change no matter what their apparent omnipotent power; nothing is static. If you are mindful, you will know exactly when to change, a how that change should happen.

Affirmation: "I am mindful to the messages of the universe calling me towards my destiny."

Love and Romance

This is not the best time to enter a brand new love relationship, simply because you have very conflicting feelings at the moment. In fact you are in a very emotional state of mind and if you go into a new relationship right now you could attract someone who is excessively needy, and this could lead to a relationship with a lot of emotional control and manipulation.

This is certainly a month when absence makes the heart grow fonder and a period apart from a partner, because you are both working very hard or travelling, can be just what the relationship needs to create a little bit of distance and perspective. This month is one in which issues easily become cloudy and confusing and therefore a little bit of space to regain balance within you own emotions can be important in order to conduct the relationship in a more sensible way. It can be very easy to become emotionally excessive or to blow things out of proportion this month, and that's why you need a little bit of distance.

Your creativity is stimulated and you your imagination is fired up, meaning romance and fantasy is more important in new and existing relationships. In new relationships there's an emphasis on feelings, fantasy, escapism and romance, you will throw other considerations out of the window, often recklessly.

You should be cautious in dating or sexual relationships now, as you want to see the most positive outcome when evaluating the potential and may not be as concerned with the consequences.

Career and Aspiration

This is an excellent month for you to work with people and focus on the softer side of you business. So the key aims for you in career are to improve the way you work with people, to increase the level of negotiation inclusively and the resilience of your business relationships, you should express concern for colleagues and be more willing to listen to other people's ideas or concerns.

It's important for you not to be dismissive of the input of others, the more you show appreciation and the more you reward those you work with with compliments and recognition, the better the team spirit and the final results.

It's very important for you to be patient in terms of your goals, particularly creative and managerial goals, because often things you do now not do not bear fruit immediately, in fact often what you do right now can feel like a failure, but in time it can end up being a triumph. So it's all about sticking to the plan, maintaining good relationships and keeping the faith.

You are more inspired and you will believe that you have an important message to convey, and if you are socially or politically minded this is an awesome time for getting out your message as you are more likely to influence people.

This is a time when you travel more, talk more and have more meaningful interactions with people who can change you as much as you change them.

You can be a little arrogant this month, but that's a missed opportunity as if you are alert you can obtain significant information in March that can mark a new direction in the way that you work or process information.

Adventure and Motivation

This is a great month for you to be more active and to express yourself on the sports field, so going to sports matches or attending exciting live competitive events can be a way of increasing you adrenaline and you appreciation for life.

Getting involved in mentoring and coaching roles whether you are coaching people in a sporting sense, or being a life coach can bring you a great amount of satisfaction.

You enjoy leading and showing others what you can do, so any arena where you get out in front and inspire people, or help motivate other people, is beneficial in terms of your own sense of confidence and helpful for the team too.

Authority figures can be a source of discouragement or obstacles and you have to diplomatically work around them. Anything which no longer cuts mustard has to go, you must focus and show determination and it's amazing what you can achieve despite the odds being stacked against you.

Validation and confidence must always be sought within and while you will garner support from friends, cheerleaders and those who align with your cause, when push comes to shove you must be able to dig deep and tap into your faith in you and what you stand for. Goals that do not matter on a deep level fall away but those which do matter cling to you and will not let you go even when you want to walk away.

Marriage and Family

It's very important for Aquarius to use your emotional intelligence in relationships, what is going on at a subtle level is not always obvious and you shouldn't use a sledgehammer to crack a nut. It's important to be non-confrontational and non-aggressive, if in doubt you should stay silent and wait for things to develop, the worst thing you can do now is to try and force situations or encourage communication if you partner is not ready.

It's important for you to go with the flow and take an understanding and patient approach to things in love. In relationships that are going well, this is an excellent time to enjoy the arts, movies and music together, it can be a romantic time, but it should also be a quiet time of reflection rather than a time to engage in very active stressful events. So while it's a romantic time, there should be no pressure for romance as such, romance should develop organically through quiet periods of reflection and togetherness.

This month you will experience a different level of understanding in your relationships and romantic interactions. Different in the sense that you experience unexpected emotions and scenarios, some of which are quite enticing and some are more baffling.

You have a better sense of the meaning of love and although your vision of what your relationship should be is a little idealistic, it's aspirational and it generates more excitement and compassion which is quite a good thing.

Money and Romance

During March you have to be very careful with you finances, you should avoid major decisions and you need to be aware of the detail and the hidden clauses in any contract you go into. This is not a time to invest in any equipment, assets or stocks because you cannot be quite sure what you're getting. If you do buy any products you should ensure that there is a money back guarantee and sufficient guarantees and warranties.

You must be careful of being idealistic in the way you spend your money, while you could be inspired to donate to charities or spend money on causes - because you are quite generous and altruistic this month - even these may not yield the results that you wish for. It's best for you to take a neutral approach to money, to keep emotion out of all you investment decisions and to be very cautious.

Living and Loving to the Full

In romantic relationships this is an excellent time to get closer, to become more physically affectionate with each other and to enjoy each other's company, however it is a time when Aquarius needs to focus on subtle forms of communication, body language, eye contact and mirroring and to lessen your reliance on the verbal side of relationships.

This can be a revealing time in relationships: couples who genuinely get each other on an emotional or a spiritual level thrive, but couples whose relationships are based on superficial attraction or tick box traits are probably going to find there is a gulf in understanding and a lot of confusion.

For all couples there's the chance this month to deepen the relationship and you guys could do that by actually watching movies or reading literature together which encourages you both to express yourselves emotionally in response to what you've seen in the film or read in the literature. So often the arts can open a door to conversation about emotional matters which will increase understanding longer term.

Planetary Cautions

This is not a good time for stock market activity, speculative financial ventures or currency trading.

Dating, double dates and joining dating apps is a mistake.

You need to be aware of where sympathy ends and love begins and you must acknowledge when you are in a business or romantic relationship out of sympathy or emotional attachment rather than love or a productive business raison d'etre.

Moon Magic

The new moon phase extends from the 21st of March to the 6th of April, this waxing phase is the perfect fortnight for new initiatives, setting plans, establishing goals, starting anything prospective and being proactive. This is the action phase, details below:

The waxing phase is not good for home improvements. Property and real estate matters are not favored. Not the best waxing period for large family events, entertaining and celebrations. Renovations and adaptation of the home is not advisable. Not successful for new business involving catering, hospitality and the environment.

This is a suitable time for exams, learning and multitasking. Great for communication projects, IT and website changes and mass media communications. Short trips for business and pleasure are favored. Good for ongoing long distance relationships and dating apps. An excellent waxing period for negotiation and making new contracts.

New artistic ventures and self-expression are less successful. Dating and social activities organized to meet potential partners are not successful. Not favorable for competitive sports and or coaching teams. New business involving children is not advisable. Creativity and invention is more difficult. Not great for launching artistic or entertainment projects to the public. Not favorable for business involving leisure and fun.

Not a good time for advertising and promotions. Self-improvement goals and motivating others is less successful. Academic studies and teaching are not favored.

Not an ideal time to travel internationally or create new import, export deals. New academic writing and publishing should not be pursued. Social or community projects are difficult.

APRIL

Essence and Energies - Faster than the speed of light

The essence this month is one of seeking thrills and making spills, but you have the break eggs to make omelet.

The tempo of this month is fast and while your energy is high you have to try and be more subtle as you are quite opinionated and not always willing to listen to others as you are rather impatient.

There may be more short journeys in connection with sudden work related opportunities. You certainly need to respond deftly to opportunities because they come and go quickly and you have to show some flexibility to get out and grab them.

This is a very productive month and you can achieve a lot and yet there may be some damage done to relations with coworkers or even family members as you take quite a strong stance and can be ruthless in you zeal to get things done. You will argue if necessary and you are a fearsome debater.

The essence this month is urgency, they say there is nothing more urgent than an idea whose time has come as that's how you feel this month. There's the irresistible urge within you to explore new ideas and spread what you find.

Affirmation: "Following the truth is not always easy but it's vital to my Aquarius destiny."

Love and Romance

You have to watch out for the mirage effect in love, all that glitters is not gold; you can idealistic about your friendships and may overstate their romantic potential in your mind. Sudden sexual liaisons with friends are possible – you are easily turned on, and you may make a move on a long-term friend; this often does not work out, but it could well suit you both temporarily.

This can be a tricky time for new relationships in which you have very different outlooks politically, religiously and regarding world view – while you may have been able to ignore these gaps in understanding so far, now you are coming up against issues which tend to be informed by belief.

You are both sensitive and impressionable in love, love right now really is blind and it can be stupid, as you are not always as discerning as you should be. You are attracted to impossible relationships and yet you often need to feel as if these are meant to be. You may fall for people who cannot offer you much, but with whom you feel an odd kinship. However, you are displaying a vulnerable side of yourself and that can leave you open to needy people or people who want to take advantage, often these two combine in certain personality types. You may choose to keep new relationships very private, perhaps some part of you knows that your friends and family would warn you off, and you do not want to hear that.

Career and Aspiration

Your ability to see the bigger picture and understand the social and political factors at play is an advantage for you.

This is an excellent month for sales, PR and promotional activities and you may be more busy with these than usual. Short trips to promote products or teach others are favored. An excellent month for improving you websites and for doing social media marketing.

Networking activities pick up pace and are more successful, you are likely to meet a diverse range of people and to exchange interesting and relevant information.

You are skilled at debate and can learn a huge amount without much stress. This energies this month help you to thrive in a dynamic, fact paced environment and are excellent for starting a new job.

It's good to use cross promotion this month, perhaps your friends or fellow business owners can promote your goods alongside theirs, and you can do likewise. It's is important to look to at where you can piggy back off the goodwill, email lists or web traffic of those in your community or network who have complimentary products. While building traffic and SEO takes time, you can often benefit from other established websites by buying space on their site, writing a guest post on their site or even getting interviewed on their YouTube channel. Reach out to other entrepreneurs and see what you can offer them in exchange for some exposure on their platforms, it helps if you are connected by geography or niche.

Adventure and Motivation

This month you feel more in control, more proactive and more capable of dealing with obstacles and hurdles. This is an excellent time to start an ambitious new project, and it's a good time for you to think big and to explore creatively an expansively. Thinking big leads to acting in a way that draws abundance to you.

Activities which are adventurous and outdoorsy in nature are favored, and you can get a lot of pleasure from competitive, leisure and also socially orientated activities. In many cases you may enjoy creating new groups and organizations with a social or community orientated purpose. You like rallying people to a cause or spearheading long term projects.

This is a great time for expanding you awareness of you social power and that can mean traveling, studying, reading or talking to others about philosophical and political subjects.

While this month brings out you generous, magnanimous side, you must be careful not to over spend, or overestimate the potential of a new project.

Marriage and Family

Relationships are very dynamic this month and the opportunity exists for progress, reconciliation, truth speaking and fun. However, you guys have to be flexible, people change, and the relationship changes, and so Aquarius needs to ask yourself if you need to alter your attitudes to reflect where the relationship is now rather than where it was ten years ago, etc.

Your desire nature is very powerful right now, and you can be hard to satisfy sexually and emotionally – this is a problem for couples who are more isolated, i.e., new in a town or country with a smaller social circle and no family around as you have to be all things all the time to each other, and that's emotionally exhausting. In this case, you need to take the lead regarding being mature and allowing things to develop organically without piling on pressure. You both need to find more pleasure outside of the relationship (not regarding having an affair obviously, but via social or creative pursuits) and you will find that satisfaction in life overall improves and you both have more positive energy to plough back into the relationship.

Money

This month is an auspicious one for starting up any business which you intend to run from home – even if only initially. It is ideal for businesses which start off with a relatively small investment and grow organically. It is important for you to try things out on a trial and error basis as you may feel constrained by limitations that are imagined – you need to work things out by experimenting or testing what can and cannot be done. In many cases, you are exploring new ground, and there may be no valuable data or evidence which can give you an indication of how to proceed. You should not toss out any idea without trying it as the unexpected can work out right now and certain limiting factors may not prove as problematic as you think.

Living and Loving to the Full

In April, they key is for you and you partner to develop friendships with positive couples who enhance your lives, support you both and encourage you to be better people. It's time to move away from troubled couples who bring negativity into your lives and drain you with their bad attitudes, bad habits or problems.

You must remember that you and you partner are the sum of, or a reflection of, the five people you spend the most time with, so have a look at who those five people are? Are they a good or bad influences? A better relationship is all about better influences in your immediate environment. So take your immediate contacts, friends and family, seriously and adjust accordingly.

Planetary Cautions

You should avoid hot and spicy food and fast foods. You need to drink loads of pure water and freshly prepared foods.

This month you need to pay attention to your health. You need to increase vitamin C and Zinc as you are more prone to infections and head colds. Allergies may flare up and so eat locally produced honey and reduce your gluten intake. Keep an alcohol diary as it's very easy to drink more than you intended to, as you don't have much of a grasp of time this month, and you lose track of the number of glasses of vino that went down the hatch.

You must be careful with machinery and tools or working with fire.

Teamwork should be avoided, unless you're a team leader.

While it's a good month for improving health with exercise and diet, you should avoid extreme and sudden changes or going cold turkey.

You must manage you work life balance carefully as you're easily stressed.

Moon Magic

The new moon phase extends from the 20th of April to the 5th of May this waxing phase is the perfect fortnight for new initiatives, setting plans, establishing goals, starting anything prospective and being proactive. This is the action phase, details below:

The waxing phase is still good for journalism, writing projects and communication with clients, customers or the public. Excellent for exams and learning new skills. A good time for IT projects. Short distance travel and internet dating is favored. A good time for social media marketing.

A great waxing phase for marriage and engagement. Also an excellent time for persuasion. Teamwork is important. Negotiations speed up and it's a great time to share ideas and work with others on problem solving. This is an energetic time in love that's perfect for working goals and challenges and putting your heads together to improve your marriage in practical ways. A favorable time for new business partnerships, legal battles or getting advice from experts.

Mercury goes retrograde in Taurus on the 21st meaning the start of a more confusing time for family matters and real estate deals are not favored. This is less favorable for planning family events, house hunting and home improvements. This period is suitable for work from home initiatives and also doing private research. This favors deep thinking, reflection and a life audit. It's also suitable for in-depth family discussions, but not reaching definite conclusions.

Essence and Energies – _"**When you want it the most there's no easy way out**_
**When you're ready to go and your heart's left in doubt**
**Don't give up on your faith"**

The essence of this month is breaking new ground, during this month it's important to break some ties with the past. Now while the first few months of the year it was important for you to nurture and appreciate all the things that have brought you to where you are, this month it's important to know when to let go, so moving on and moving on up are very important.

This is an excellent month for breaking old habits and patterns that have enslaved you and breaking free, however sometimes it's also good to reestablish roots or patterns that you feel have been beneficial. So it's important for you to have the awareness to understand what in life you need to take you forward, and what would be an important foundation or Launchpad for the New You that you are building, and also what's holding you back. Often the wisdom this month is in knowing the difference between what you need and what you need rid of.

So this month is not about throwing the baby out with bathwater, it's more about having a good understanding of where you want to be, what's holding you back and then having the courage to leave certain things behind.

At a deep level you are undergoing a unconscious revolution and since your unconscious mind has a powerful effect on your view of reality, your whole experience of the world is going to be quite different and this month is a point in case.

Affirmation: "Change is the only constant in life and I chose to evolve into a better future."

Love and Romance

Jupiter Transits Pluto in Aquarius by square which increases sexual desire and you may crave more fulfilment from your sex life, so this provides the inventive to have intimate conversations and possibly seek medical advice to improve sex life. If you're single you may get into relationships that are all about sex, but which can also be controlling and toxic.

It's difficult for you to be patient and your partner may feel you're egotistical and demanding, to be honest you can be hard work during this phase, but you're dealing with many internal and external obstacles and you will eventually make sense of and overcome them.

This is often a time of powerful psychological encounters with people, this can be with your partner or someone you who enters into your life. Very often a person in your life tends to get under your skin, it may be someone you've just met or maybe your partner is just behaving in a way that is particularly erratic or irrational and it's really getting to you. It could be that you are obsessively drawn to someone who tends to push your buttons.

However, whatever it is that is getting you hot under the collar, it's important to get in touch with your emotions this month. It's quite enlivening to be a little bit angry, impulsive or impetuous, because this helps jump you out of comfort zones and gets the adrenaline going. Often a little bit adrenaline is what we all need to push us into a new phase of life.

Career and Aspiration

You need to double down and be uncompromising, this is a time to take the baton and run with it, you shouldn't delay and you must ensure you press home an advantage.

Increased intensity means that you are more likely to reach goals and targets especially if you're emotionally involved the project.

This can be a period of increased popularity and the ability to relate to people and develop good public relations in you work. You may receive added support from you parents or family members and family life in general play a more important part in the decisions you make in you work life.

Adventure and Motivation

Jupiter entering Taurus this month facilitates home moves, home improvements and investment in property. You may have the desire to move somewhere bigger or perhaps to move to a place which offers more freedom or allows you greater space and flexibility.

This is an excellent time for clear outs and decluttering. It's important for you to tidy you home and home office and start again with a feeling of being unencumbered.

This is also an exciting time to research Feng Shui and understand how more thoughtful redecorating and home organizing can free up energy and remove outer chaos which promotes inner chaos. Tidy house, tidy mind.

Energy flows within or without are important considerations in terms of well-being and family harmony.

This is a fantastic month for using positive affirmations and for exploring mind power. During this month the power of attraction works particularly strongly, and it's vital - if you are to be successful

- that you don't neglect the mental and emotional element of any task.

It's important to work with a full appreciation of who you are and what you stand for, so when your practical goals align with a spiritual purpose you can be that much more effective.

It's important to use your your spidey senses and your intuition, so while you should be ambitious and assertive when it comes to showing leadership in your job or being more independent in the way you live your life and pursue your goals, you should also be very aware of hidden agendas and of vested interests.

This is a time to be optimistic and positive, but also a time to be weary and a little bit cynical. You shouldn't be naive, there is a big difference between being in a positive frame of mind and being deluded, so it's important that you factor everything in, pay attention to details and make sure you understand the mindsets of your opponents. So this is all about thinking and outwitting other people on your road to success.

Marriage and Family

This may not be a good time to start arguments or enter a situation where you feel exposed, or are likely to be criticized as you are more vulnerable and sensitive right now.

This is a month of sudden turbulence and disruption. It's almost like you are taking a plane flight and all of a sudden you've had some bad weather and the plane is rocking and rolling, this turbulence will most likely surface in your personal life and any problems or tensions that you have refused to deal with until now can come to the fore. If you've been acknowledging your need for renewal in your life and dealing with the problems, you might preempt much of the disruption of this month. In this case, it might be an incredibly exciting month where you can creatively harness your energy and make bold changes to your home and family life that will put everyone on a better course for the future.

Some frustration and challenge is to be expected on a personal level. It's often a time of misunderstandings in relationships, probably because you are both being less objective or are confused. In fact, you and you partner are probably giving each other mixed messages, so you must try hard to communicate clearly or walk away and allow the dust to settle.

This energies this month can lead to some problems as you can be reactionary and excessive but not predictable. Life may be like an emotional rollercoaster and you may overreact to certain situations using a sledgehammer to crack a nut.

If you and you partner are usually assertive people, this month could lead you guys to become overbearing and controlling or even oppressive towards each other. However, if you guys can identify real problems and root causes and aim your focus at these, this is a wonderful time to take back your power and start rewriting the script for your life.

Money and Finance

This is a good building phase and you should focus on taking projects forward and adding to what you have already achieved. This is a time of consolidation and moving forward in a systematic way. Your confidence often increases because you will have certain amount of success during this month and will feel rewarded for hard work done.

You must be in control of you unconscious, as old habits and subconscious attitudes can tend to affect you adversely, so being successful with money is contingent on changing poor habits or thought patterns into more positive ones.

You tend to be more excitable right now and can jump the gun. You must avoid financial decisions as they may be made based on feelings, which are running high, rather than good financial data.

Living and Loving to the Full

Psychologically it is important for you to have conversations with yourself, get to acknowledge your feelings and understand where they are coming from. Aquarius often tend to gloss over important internal matters as you mask every problem with busyness and mental distraction, a dynamic and fast paced life style can be you way of avoiding yourself and your deeper issues.

This is an ideal month to spend some time alone to get in touch with your emotions. You could even have a good cry to release any 'stuff' which has built up. Watching a good movie or listening to music that triggers you emotionally could help you let it all out. You should reconsider yet not dwell on the past, but understand better why it matters and release it.

Dealing with internal issues helps growth and better romantic interactions.

Planetary Cautions

The Mercury retrograde until the 15th affects your 4th house and the sphere of family is highlighted.

This is not a good time to move, house hunt or buy property.

This retrograde happens in an 'emotional' and deep house. This once again gives you cause to think deeply, to mull over and indeed to brood. You can be quite obsessed with the past. A degree of self-pity and inevitability is connected to this transit as well as the other retrogrades. You may not be very positive or forward looking during this phase as it encourages nostalgic or even mawkish behavior.

You may well have a mini reset where you suddenly have realizations that cast new light in recent issues, especially family matters.

Important decisions may have to be made about family and these shouldn't be rushed as facts are slow to come to light and you guys should not jump the gun. In some cases erratic behavior from other of you family members may disrupt your lives.

Moon Magic

The new moon phase extends from the 19th of May to the 3rd of June this waxing phase is the perfect fortnight for new initiatives, setting plans, establishing goals, starting anything prospective and being proactive. This is the action phase, details below:

A good waxing phase for learning new skills and refining and perfecting you projects or written work. Client feedback is important. Better communication with colleagues and the people you serve is important. You may need a second opinion on medical matters. A good time for medical research to investigate better health solutions. Great for new diets and fitness regimes.

Excellent for romantic liaisons, dating, double dates, social activities and arranging parties. Suitable for competitive activities and self-promotion. Good for entertainment and leisure businesses. Dealing with children as a parent or teacher is favored.

The waxing phase is great for trying new things, meeting new people or going to new places. Excellent period for new health and fitness initiatives. Sports and competitive activities are favored. Ideal for personal goals and being assertive. Excellent for debate and presenting ideas or making a good first impression.

Caution is needed in dealing with debt and financial matters. A time to be wary of getting a loan, extending credit to clients or organizing a grant. Income from donations, subscriptions and royalties is unreliable.

A time to be cautious yet proactive about financial reorganization.

JUNE

Essence and Energies – Breaking the spell

This month is important for working on your self-esteem and your ability to shape your life with more assertiveness.

Circumstances can throw a light on any lack of self-esteem or self-worth which allow you to stay in situations which are really not conducive to your growth. Now we all know Aquarius as a free spirit who is idealistic and spontaneous and yet as a fixed sign you are liable to fall into predictable yet limiting patterns. So you can be the spoke in the wheels of your own future, where you accept less that the best now in the belief that in the long run that will all change, and yet without direct effort it may very well not. You cannot drift on in the faith that the winds of providence will blow you to your destiny.

This month you must grapple with yourself to release the hand brake and really crack on with making the dreams reality, but with patient and deliberate action. You need to take a look at self-worth issues and you will begin to understand your relationships better and how you perhaps take a lot more than you should, this begins a process of rebalancing your needs with the needs of others. Your priorities in relationships and work change and you may want to redefine the way you guys relate and the day to day functioning of being together or working.

Affirmation: "The future is not an accident, it's being designed by me right now through my actions and attitudes."

Love and Romance

You're not happy when you are put on the spot or coerced into making decisions which you're not ready for. You can be rather evasive this month and will strongly resist being bossed around or controlled. You are looking for growth and evolvement within the relationship, and where you partner is too set in their ways or too staid in their approach there will be problems.

You're in a very outgoing phase of life where you welcome novelty; if you partner is happy to embrace this, then all the better for your relationship. If your partner is agro to your freedom loving, adventure seeking bent then you guys will drift apart (not necessarily permanently) this month. You're impatient with routine and with pettiness; you wants to reject all those trivial aspects of day-to-day life and see a bigger, more promising picture.

This is such a great year for Aquarius moving forward, accepting that some problems cannot be solved, only outgrown, and the major stumbling block can be a partner who is still immersed in the very problems and trivialities you want to leave behind. Another excellent month for single Aquarius to experience new people for fun and love, but without the pressure of commitment.

Career and Aspiration

You may get a little down on yourself this month and feelings of despair and inadequacy may dog you. However, you're very idealistic right now, and you may have been somewhat unrealistic, and so instead of feeling downhearted, you need a more down to earth appraisal of how things are going, after which you will see they are not so bad at all. This month you're inclined to be very distracted and dreamy, it is not such a good month to deal with practical matters. It is, however, a wonderful month to deal with subjects that require imagination, inspiration and insight. You may also be driven to travel in order to volunteer or sacrifice your time for those who are in desperate need. You have a very strong desire to reach out to others.

You're extremely imaginative and creative right now, you can excel in any field where a flow of ideas or brainstorming is required. June is a superb time for artists, poets, photographers, designers or writers. Photographers or cinematographers can create images more powerful than words. This is also a wonderful time for those Aquarius who teach – you can inspire enthusiasm and interest, and put across complex concepts and theories.

Adventure and Motivation

If you're in a building phase of a new project now, the difficulty is that some of the work you're doing feels as if it is at odds with the end goal. It can be hard to hold the vision while the groundwork is still ongoing – you must keep the faith in yourself and your goal. The long hours you put in now will begin to show dividends. Yielding to the needs and wants of colleagues, co-workers or interests groups should not be seen as a sign of weakness, but rather as your secret weapon this month.

You are quite forceful and highly resilient, and that gives you a great deal of power as you are not easily deterred. Events this June can shape your character and this is a key time in your life as certain character traits which come to the fore now are strongly indicative of future directions.

It may be a sudden crisis which demands decisive and courageous action, or an exciting but daunting opportunity you face which suddenly unleashes a spirit of adventure and also of conquest and confrontation. You are more aware of and accepting of parts of your personality which you may have denied or avoided before, and those neglected or unconscious traits now become key assets. It's like you opened up your tool box and found some sharp and shiny tools you had forgotten you had, and by finding them again, you get a whole new zest for your work.

Marriage and Family

There is an emphasis on entertaining in the home and on social gatherings with friends and family. You are feeling warm-hearted and generous right now, and that bodes well for sex and love in the relationship. Aquarius are highly passionate and amorous in the bedroom and will demand an equal response from their partners. Touching and physical intimacy, especially if it is spontaneous is what you're craving, and you will be happy to make the first move.

You're very giving emotionally and is happy to talk about your partner's problems and help soothe and inspire her.

If you and your partner have a clear set goals and are able to work together, then this is an excellent month for fighting against adversity or achieving important objectives together.

However, in all relationships adversity could bring you together or tear you apart, so it's all down to you. It's likely that you as a couple will face some adversity, but you should unite together against the threats and use it as an opportunity to become stronger, to work on your team work and to let the strength that you have within the relationship shine through.

In weaker relationships you may allow the adversity to tear you apart as you turn on each other rather than focusing on the enemy or issues at hand.

The energy from Mars brings a great deal of fire power to your relationship and this can be used to start challenging new goals that can take your relationship in a positive new direction. It's also a time when you should reintroduce a little bit of passion and excitement into the relationship, there's no excuse to be boring, so be creative about the way you show each other affection and love.

Money and Finance

Issues to do with financing and insuring projects may be the problem, or it could be getting more cash injected into you department. Plans are on ice until you can restructure some of the details. Your judgment on matters of financial importance is key, and many of you decisions will come under scrutiny later on, and so you should take you time and be sure. Diligent preparation with some bold decisions is what is called for; you will not be afraid to stick your neck out, but should be prepared to answer for it and defend you actions. You may not always be in the right place at the right time this month, but you should do not let that frustrate you, you must just keep working around the problems and improvising.

Living and Loving to the Full

Single Aquarius can win over or impress a potential lover or new love interest this month by impressing them with wit, conversation, knowledge and skill. You should show off what you know and show what a fascinating and well-informed person you are. You should take a fresh approach to looking for a partner by engaging in new social activities, including pub quizzes, charity runs, fetes, film clubs, etc. You're in a rather flirty mood and should have no shortage of potential partners to impress – that does not mean you will immediately settle for one, you may even keep a few on the go while you decide. In marriages and permanent partnerships, you may annoy you partner by seeming erratic. You're in a playful mood and are not erratic at all, just restless and inclined to inject some much-needed fun and spontaneity into the relationship. This month you will do your best to avoid conflict and heavy emotional conversations, it's all about enjoyment and having fun again and rediscovering what it was like when you relationship was new.

Planetary Cautions

This is not a good month for real estate deals or home improvements. Inviting family to stay is also not advisable.

There is a high degree of unpredictability within the home environment and so any plans made quickly fall apart of have to be changed radically.

You may have to deal with sudden events or mishaps at home and so you should ensure you insurance is up to date.

Family members may act erratically or let you down.

Home hunting may be fun, but not much of importance can be gained.

Moon Magic

The new moon phase extends from the 18th of June to the 3rd of July this waxing phase is the perfect fortnight for new initiatives, setting plans, establishing goals, starting anything prospective and being proactive. This is the action phase, details below:

The waxing phase is great for you spiritual growth, achieving resolution and for contemplating. Meditation and mindfulness are successful. Great period for going on retreats and enjoying you own company. A great time for inspirational and artistic ventures. Positive visualization and affirmations it prayer are important activities.

Excellent for charitable and humanitarian work.

Things tend to be confusing in terms of business negotiations, mediation and legal matters, and you should avoid concrete decisions on outsourcing or recruitment.

Brand new activities and fresh starts in uncharted territory aren't favored. A good time for physical activities, getting fitter or improving physical health with physiotherapy, reiki, acupuncture or chiropractic therapy.

The waxing period favors money matters, getting loans, rearranging debt and improving you financial position. It's favorable for all business involving audit, accounting and tax. It's also perfect for discussions about financial planning in marriage.

This waxing phase is good for learning, exams and writing or journalistic projects. Short getaways are favored. IT projects, sales and marketing are successful.

JULY

Essence and Energies – Orpheus in the Underworld

The Essence this month is otherworldly and alternative ways of thinking and as you are naturally drawn to the whole alternative sphere and you have a great interest in astrology, metaphysics and alternative ways of understanding your life and the universe, this is an excellent month for you to explore things like spirituality, acupuncture, yoga or meditation.

It can be a great distraction from the more mundane and immediate concerns to explore the hidden depths of existence and you may even have experiences that are more profound and quite revealing.

This can be a time of digging beneath the surface and asking difficult questions both of yourself and of the world. It's a time of the 'apocalypse' which literally means and lifting the veil, so you need to have the courage to delve courageously into subject matters that could be a little bit shocking or could change your whole view because this is the key to growth right now.

At a deep level the mysteries of life and death are not abstractions to you anymore, they feel important and relevant and that's why you need to be able to understand this sphere and you may even do things like a visit a psychic or a clairvoyant because you want to tap into some sort of energy to give you a slightly different take on your life.

Affirmation: "I allow my higher self to guide me and help me make sense of my life path."

Love and Romance

This is an excellent month for new relationships, love and romance.

It's certainly a time when you should try to be more active socially as it's likely that you could meet suitable dates at dinner parties, blind dates and double dates. The most effective new relationships are ones where you prospective partner is already a family friend or friend of a friend, so often you don't have to look far beyond your circles to meet someone suitable.

In your relationships, you should jump right and you shouldn't be too cautious, you shouldn't mince you words and you should really express yourself and look to have fun in a vibrant new and daring relationship.

Relationships get off to the best start where there's a lot of honesty, straightforwardness and a free flow of communication. If you feels a new relationship is a little bit stilted, or a partner is standoffish, then this is not off to a good start, the chemistry should be obvious immediately and if it isn't the relationship isn't on.

Career and Aspiration

This month in career it's all about careful analysis and being more organized. It's very important for you to take a systematic and methodical approach to work and it's also very important for you to shut out distractions. Right now there can be a little bit of a hubbub in the office, and a lot of people are talking but not getting on with what's really important. Your strength this month is that you understand what to do and are capable of putting the plans together, but the only problem is you don't get a lot of support from others and you can often feel a little bit isolated, so you need to stick to your principles and go with your analysis and yoru instincts without being put off by others.

During this month details are really important and cannot be ignored, but sometimes the details can also be misleading so it's important for you not to lose sight of the bigger picture. If things don't make sense, this is a cause for you to investigate further because you may be onto something that everyone else is going to miss and this could be a unique opportunity.

Adventure and Motivation

In terms of your private and social life, this is an excellent time for renewing friendships and relationships, you may enjoy going to a reunion or reconnecting with people from you past. This is an excellent time to work on you family relationships and fostering better understanding, and if there has been any ill-feeling or disputes within the family arena, this is an excellent time to get a dialogue going and start communicating again.

It is a certainly an excellent time for reconciliation and for healing, and the key to doing this is through re-engaging and exchanging views. This is definitely not a time when you need to feel as if you have to agree with, or get on with everyone, as the whole idea is that everyone should be able to get things off their chest, have their say and a healing process can be begun even if it doesn't finish this month.

In general, entertaining in your home, holding events or dinner parties at home or coordinating social activities from you home, bring a lot of satisfaction and fun to your life.

This is definitely a time when you can be more involved with spiritual activities with revolutionary aspects of society. It's a time when you might be quite politically aware, you may be getting involved with activism or trying to counteract narrow ways of thinking and helping other people to seek new avenues and approaches for the truth.

Marriage and Family

This is a month where Aquarius and your partner will have to thrash out issues to do with money. It is more than likely that you and your partner will not be seeing eye to eye in terms of how to manage your financial future or on important decisions regarding money and loans.

This is definitely a month where you both tend to have your egos in the mix and it's important that Aquarius take a step back, and you both make the right decision rather than trying to be right.

Rather than arguing about money, you should both be talking about what you feel the biggest threats and priorities going forward are, because often it's not so much the finances you are arguing about, it's down to differences in what you both think is most pressing, most important or most problematic. So in order to address your money problems, it's probably best first to do some sort of analysis on what the most immediate problems or priorities are facing you both are, and go from there, because this creates a context for the action plan.

Money and Finance

This month Aquarius feels a lot of urgency in terms of tackling any financial issues or problems, and this can often lead you into disputes with you partner, as I have discussed, however it's a great thing that you're on it and looking to resolve issues and this certainly is a month not to shy away or hide from difficult decisions.

This month you're ready to bite the bullet, you are quite determined and courageous in the way you tackles problems and the key is 'do it now'. Often being a little bit daring and taking a few risks pays off, so while I'm not suggesting you should be speculative or gamble with money, if you works harder and thinks out the box and takes a risk in terms of an unconventional approach, this can stand you in good stead.

Living and Loving to the Full

This is an excellent month for sexual awareness, it may be a good idea for you to think about what is most fulfilling and exciting for you sexually, and then to see how far you current sex life falls short. We can't get what we want if we don't know what we want, so often it may be a good idea for you and you partner to explore some new ideas gently and lovingly in an intimate arena to find out if you guys are missing a trick.

It's very often the case that couples lose confidence or interest in the bedroom simply because it's become routine boring, or because one or both don't feel satisfied, and it's difficult to broach the subject, but this is a month where discussion about your sex life should be on the table, and you may want to use some erotic books or sexy movies to help stimulate your desire and reinvigorate your sexual imagination.

Planetary Cautions

This is a time to avoid confrontation you shouldn't look to initiate any legal disputes or proceedings, it's best to pursue mediation and reconciliation as far as possible.

In arguments, you should try and hold your tongue as you're likely to regret saying things later on. You should not jump to conclusions and should try and be as fair-minded as possible, even in heated debates. Arguing and getting angry will not really get you anywhere, as this is not a month where an argument clears the air, it's a month where you need to keep trying and keep remembering what each of you guys said in the argument in terms of what you need and expect from each other.

It is often your private and personal life that is under the most scrutiny and subject the most change right now, and at a fundamental level you need to re-adjust your compass. So this is a time when you can feel a little bit insecure or restless, often because the things that are familiar to you and which you've relied upon are either no longer there or are changing, and so it's a case of looking for a whole new way to find security and stability in your life and this may be in a slightly less traditional way.

Moon Magic

The new moon phase extends from the 17th of July to the 30th of July this waxing phase is the perfect fortnight for new initiatives, setting plans, establishing goals, starting anything prospective and being proactive. This is the action phase, details below:

The waxing phase is great for new career directions, business management, leadership, PR and public engagement. Pioneering action, reputational improvement and being head hunted is possible.

The waxing phase is not ideal for marriage and engagement. New business partnerships are not successful. Not great for getting advice from experts.

Retreats and spiritual pursuits like mindfulness and meditation are less successful. Not a great time to do charitable work. Dealing with government agencies and large corporations is very tricky.

AUGUST

Essence and Energies – "You sexy thing!"

This is an ideal month to feel more sexy, to pamper yourself and to embrace your feminine energy. This is a wonderful time to go for a spa treatment, if money allows, or get a brand new hairstyle, spray tan and manicure or something that you can make you feel fabulous and feminine.

A lot of this year has been about embracing change, adjusting to new circumstances, reviewing your future etc. but this is definitely a month for relaxation, enjoyment and doing all the things that make you feel glamorous and special.

It's also a time to revel in sensual pleasures. Now Aquarius is an air sign and of course you're inspired by ideas, by debate, by communications with people etc. but right now I want you to appreciate everything that's early from beautiful smells, textures, sounds and tastes, and therefore you should indulge in doing things in a beautiful environment, exploring artistic delights and visual delights and appreciating music and good food.

This is a month when you should indulge yourself in wine, chocolate and song.

Affirmation: "I deserve the best in life and I pamper myself with sensual pleasures to renew and recharge my soul."

Love and Romance

This is quite a karmic time in love, people whom you attract now are likely to be people with whom you have a past life connection, and therefore the relationship may be more complicated because of the past life karma trying to work its way through in this life.

Even if new relationships are difficult and quite provocative, you should try and stick with it and understand what about yourself you're learning through the new relationship.

Complex psychological issues tend to emerge this month when you are in love, and a new partner may bring out aspects of yourself that you're unfamiliar with or even uncomfortable with, and that's why you need to be very self-aware and understand exactly what is being triggered within you, or indeed what a partner is projecting onto you, because projection operates quite powerfully this month.

It's important to assess recent events which have worked out in a way that you didn't anticipate or may not even liked, so you can come to terms with those and understand that decisions you made and actions you took in the past were for a reason and the consequences now either have to be lived with or resolved, but either way you need to accept where you are and forge a way forward that you both agree on.

Career and Aspiration

This is a month when your relationships in business are redefined. Working closely with other people can be a double-edged sword, as on one hand it can bring certain benefits to the table which can help increase you confidence, and if you work in tandem with people who compliment your experience and skills it can be very successful. However often this month you can fall into situations where people try to dominate and control you through the strength of their personality, and this can only lead to a lot of problems and wrong directions.

This month you have to be very careful of narcissistic personalities who try and set the agenda, control the facts and force their version of events down your throat, so while often you can feel flattered and stimulated by working with powerful people, you shouldn't lose you sense of who you are, or of your integrity.

Adventure and Motivation

This month you can have a lot of fun within the family sphere, often events with you partner or with extended family are quite fulfilling and enjoyable. Again it's an excellent month for entertaining at home or maybe making some minor home improvements which aren't too costly.

You may get a lot of satisfaction out of doing things like improving you garden or DIY, alternatively you may muck in with other family members to help an older relative and in that way reinforces bonds with the older generation.

Introspection is enhanced from exploring you roots, if you live far away from where you were born, or even not so far away, you might enjoy visiting your old school, where you were born or places you've lived, just to gain a sense of where your roots are, how far you're come and the kind of influences that have shaped you. Digging into your past through ancestry research or DNA research could also be something that brings you a lot of enjoyment and fascination.

Marriage and Family

This month Venus is retrograde in you solar 7th house of marriage, this is a time of intense debate and hopefully increased understanding in relationships, there are more dilemmas and it's more important than ever to have frank honest discussions.

The problem this month is there can be some people pleasing, some holding back due to a desire to avoid conflict and some diplomacy which can actually stand in the way of progress, so while it's important to be conciliatory and kind, it's also very important not to shy away from getting to the heart of the matter, and this can only be done if you are frank with each other.

This can be an excellent phase for reconciliation, if you and your partner have been having a lot of difficulties, this is a good time for marriage counselling, however it can also be a good time to take a break and for you both to enjoy yourselves separately before you can come back together. There is a need for a clearing heads and little bit of separation can help you both to get a perspective and to dissolve any people pleasing and get beyond the barriers which can be inhibiting.

It's important to have conversations with your partner about the level of balance in the relationship. It's very easy for us to lose touch with exactly what each partner is putting in and taking out of the relationship, and at the heart of most difficulties in relationships is one partner feeling that they are putting in more and being taken for granted. So this is an excellent month to have discussions about how each of you feel about how the relationship is working out, and to lay your cards on the table. There should be an opportunity for you both to get things off your chest, especially when they relate to issues of caring and sharing. If one partner feels that the relationship has become imbalanced in terms of power or the input, now is the time to correct that.

In all relationships this should be a time where there is an open forum where you can both call each other to account for your actions, not in order to judge each other or to blame each other, but to create a sense that wrongs are being righted, and is an opportunity for you both to correct things before any aspect of the relationship deteriorates.

Money and Finance

They say you have to spend money to make money, but that can sometimes be a mistake particularly this month. It's very important for Aquarius not to try and spend yourself out of a hole, in many cases it's better to consolidate and delay in order to save money rather than throwing good money after bad.

You may feel a lot of frustration in terms of your financial situation, but it's very important for you to choose you advisers wisely as good advice this month is gold dust. However if you feel that someone is putting a lot of pressure on you to make a certain decision or sign a contract, this should be an enormous red flag as anything you do this month should be of your own free will and according to your own understanding of the facts not because of pressure.

Living and Loving to the Full

This is an excellent month to shine a light on relationships, however a focus on problems that should be fixed shouldn't be the whole enchilada. There is a need for appreciation and celebration in relationships where you get together to clink your champagne glasses and say, "Well done us!" Renewal and positivity in relationships should be cultivated, problems should be seen as opportunities to make the relationship more dynamic.

Relationships can blossom and cooperation can bring the two of you closer together as you acknowledge life's blessings.

You should use this month to cultivate an even closer connection with your life partner and if single, now is the time to step out and let yourself shine. Your positivity and radiance can be magnetic now, and thus important relationships can begin.

Planetary Cautions

You must be careful not to succumb to self-doubt and to judge yourself too severely, as this can lead to a loss of power and respect from others, which in turn leads to you missing opportunities.

You must not dither, you need to avoid overwhelming yourself with useless information or distractions.

Momentum can be easily lost this month through procrastinating and you could become anxious that you're falling behind in you plans, so it's important to stay bold and focused.

You need to forgive yourself and you also need to reject the fear of being wrong, making a mistake or being judged.

Moon Magic

The new moon phase extends from the 16th of August to the 30th of August this waxing phase is the perfect fortnight for new initiatives, setting plans, establishing goals, starting anything prospective and being proactive. This is the action phase, details below:

The waxing phase is not ideal for loans, mortgages or taking on more debt. Managing large sums of money is not advisable. Not a suitable time for tax and accounting changes. New sexual relationships aren't favored. New research and development projects are not successful.

An excellent month for new roles at work or recruitment of staff as well as traveling to attend a course. This is a successful time for new diets, innovative health initiatives and anything more strict or restrictive in terms of diet. A good time to join a gym or begin a new fitness regime. Training staff is successful. A favorable time to open a business connected to animals, manufacturing or medicine.

An excellent time for real estate business and property deals. Good for house hunting and renovation. Working from home is favored. Great for family events and celebrating. Reunions and reviving the past are helpful. Good for business involving hospitality, catering, care and the environment. Great for achieving resolution on past issues.

SEPTEMEBER

Essence and Energies – "In my imagination there is no complication."

During this month the challenge is to bring imagination to things that are a little bit boring or rather dull and predictable.

Right now it's often best to follow a structure or protocol and to do things in the tried and tested way, it's important to use your experience and play the percentages IE go with what works best and has always been successful for you. However that doesn't mean that you have to be entirely predictable, it's time to put a brand new spin and creative alternative into all your plans.

So even though it's best to continue down a familiar path rather than striking it out and doing things in a radical or an orthodox way, you can still reach the height of achievement without taking risks but just by using more imagination, more empathy and your reservoir of knowledge to deliver something that is inspired but non-threatening to the more conservative or conventional person.

So it's all about your unique ability to bring a little bit of surprise, imagination and creativity to something that has been done before and has low risk.

Affirmation: "There is always room for my magic touch."

Love and Romance

In romance, this is a month when differences in priorities and the approach you and a partner have to life become more problematic, it maybe a month when you and you partner start to have discussions about money, either because you aim to move in together or because you're spending a lot more time together and therefore need to talk about finances. It often becomes apparent this month how keen one or the other of you are, and it's highly likely that this will create some hurdles because Aquarius may be having cold feet and a partner may be wanting to surge ahead even though Aquarius could have some lingering questions.

So this month is make or break for new relationships, you will either decide that you guys don't have that much in common and the relationship is best left alone, or you will decide that it's promising, that you're intrigued and excited about it and you want to push forward, but that's going to require a little bit more commitment from you which means that you have to bite the bullet

Career and Aspiration

This is an excellent month to work on the sales and promotional side of your business, you should seek to improve you visibility and enhance your reputation by possibly being more environmentally friendly or community orientated.

It's really important right now for you to have integrity and a sense of collective responsibility in everything you do. While you are quite gung ho and ready for anything, you must be careful to include others and explain yourself adequately, because this increases the level of support that you gain from colleagues.

This is a great month for breaking the mold, trying a few things new things and just being a little bit more adventurous in the way you go about your work. It's a time to incorporate new ideas and also a good time to travel in connection with your work, with training or increasing geographical reach.

This month there are opportunities to take more responsibility when it comes to money and this can mean money management for other people, managing money for charities or humanitarian organizations or investing and tax matters.

However, often these come with hidden problems, so it's very important to have an enquiring mind and to investigate the details from the get go to uncover exactly what it all entails. Some of these opportunities will be an excellent way to gain new experiences, to increase your confidence and even to do something very good for society, however you do have to be careful of whether all these plans are properly formulated, otherwise you can be left with an awful lot more to do then you initially thought.

Adventure and Motivation

This is an excellent month for getting the adrenaline going and for engaging in sports or outdoor activities that bring you a lot of excitement.

This is a fantastic time for all sorts of competitive activities, it doesn't need to be sports, but it's great for you to get into a social setting where you can either debate or compete with others on a number of levels.

You enjoy the thrill of being amongst people and experiencing group events, you also like it when you can motivate and inspire others. So it's not only fun for you to compete, but it's also quite a lot of fun where you have to coach, support or motivate other people, because you enjoy being influential in a social setting and inspiring people to do things that are along the lines of their self-development or which are community orientated.

The battle you have to get through now is doubt and some fears, it's likely that you're starting something a little bit new and there's a tad of anxiety, but it's important to see it as an adventure, because anytime we feel a little bit unsure of our abilities or are not sure if we will succeed, it actually means that we are on the right track. As soon as you are questioning yourself and feeling uncertain, it means you will start thinking and when you are thinking, you are learning, and when you are learning, you are opening doors for yourself. So don't be discouraged by any feelings of inadequacy and doubt, embrace this as an opportunity to use your excellent problem-solving skills.

Marriage and Family

This month in marriage it's very important for you to deal with anything that is confusing, ill-defined or vague. While some problems are very obvious and can be dealt with head on, other problems lurk in the background and you're only vaguely aware of them and while they may cause you anxiety or worry, it's not easy to tackle them because you're not even sure how to go about it.

So this month it's important for you to analyze any strange fears and anxieties or premonitions that you are having, as well as anything that you are worried about in terms of your partner and you may want to start trying to get to the bottom of this, but this should not necessarily be easy.

So the key in love this month is that you have to be a little bit of a detective and you have to probe and almost preempt problems by tackling anything that is a threat, even if not a current problem to the relationship.

Money and Finance

This can be a tricky month in terms of arranging loans and financing, it is very important for you to get legal advice, to read the fine print and to be aware of all the relevant details.

The problem right now is that you tend to get conflicting advice from people, or the people that you work with in terms of business keep changing their story or are unreliable. The key right now is that you have to rely on yourself, and therefore you shouldn't delegate or be totally reliant on information from other people.

It's probably not a good month to take on managing large sums of money for others because you may not have all the relevant information, and you could be led down the garden path. This month you can't always be sure what you're getting into, so caution is advisable.

Living and Loving to the Full

This month enhancement of love magic is all about creating more security in the relationship. Often one of the big problems in love relationships is that one of the partners feels insecure and needs reassurance and the other partner may not necessarily acknowledge this. So this month it's important for Aquarius to create more certainty for you partner, and carrying on from last month, this can be about having important relationship discussions, allowing each partner to get things off their chest etc. but it's also about saying 'I love you' and doing meaningful and thoughtful things that show your partner you care, and you're engaged in a relationship.

So this month to enhance relationships what you have to do is to work on the relationship in ways that are meaningful to you partner, therefore sending out a strong message of commitment.

Planetary Cautions

Mercury retrograde until the 16th is in your eighth house. This poses difficulties for the household finances and if you guys are married or share a bank account, there can be disagreements or discord about how and where money is spent. The retrograde period indicates that debt, taxes and issues about money are top of the agenda and often recent decisions have to be scrutinized or reassessed. It's also possible that you guys will blame each other for the outcome of recent financial decisions as there is a tendency to pass the buck until the dust settles and a plan is put in place.

The eighth house is more than just money, it boils down to values and often flashpoints about money reveal deeper discord between you. This period thus require tolerance and compromise and some new relationships can fall at this hurdle as it becomes clear that you are never going to see eye to eye on important issues. It's vital for you both to be alert to what's going on at a deeper level and ask yourselves if you like what you are seeing.

This is a good period for honest discussion and for looking at your problems from a psychological point of view. Games and manipulative behavior is common during this phase, which is why you need to be alert to this and to keep everything honest. Aquarius occasionally uses emotional manipulation and very indirect methods of getting your own way and that may well be the case during this retrograde.

This is an excellent time for sex counselling or trying to improve or work through sexual issues.

Moon Magic

The new moon phase extends from the 14th of September to the 29th of September this waxing phase is the perfect fortnight for new initiatives, setting plans, establishing goals, starting anything prospective and being proactive. This is the action phase, details below:

The waxing phase is great for property matters, renovation and redecorating. Moving house or house hunting is favored. Good for a

staycation or enjoying you own history or culture.
Great for businesses involving research, conservation, food and hospitality.
Healing and forgiveness is important in the family arena. Great for travelling to family reunions. Good for researching family history.

Networking and professional events are favored. Joining new groups with a political aim is successful. Great for social media marketing or activity. This is a great waxing phase for making new friends and traveling to large events with friends and colleagues. Good for activities that are very innovative or scientific.

Good for managing money and jobs in the financial sector. Suitable for discussions about money with partners, investors or a bank. Audit and financial investigation is successful. Borrowing and financial reorganization is suitable for the waxing phase. This is a good time to begin psychological therapy

Not a suitable time for marriage and engagement. Not the best waxing phase for marriage counseling and initiatives to reignite understanding and cooperation in love are favored. Less suitable for teamwork. Not a good time to choose new advisors or professional business partners.

OCTOBER

Essence and Energies – "Uphill battle, I look good when I climb I'm ferocious, precocious, I get braggadocios"

This month the essence is the pursuit of ideas. This is a very action-oriented time and it's a good month to show commitment in terms of putting ideas into action. You are able to draw on more courage and are less likely to be fearful or reticent. This is an excellent time to jump right in, so don't hold back, charge ahead with your ideas and make things happen.

It's really good to be competitive and to get the ball rolling as your confidence will increase as you proceed, so even if you have a certain degree of insecurity or uncertainty, once the action gets going and get in the flow, your confidence and your enthusiasm will carry you through.

This is also an excellent time for any sporting competition, but in general you have a highly competitive spirit, so it's wonderful to into the fray of any activity where you can have an opportunity to prove yourself and get reward and recognition.

You should be careful not to let competitiveness become ruthlessness, help others who lack the same motivation as yourself but don't let them stand in your way.

Affirmation: "I am filled with the positive energy and enthusiasm to give life to my ideas."

Love and Romance

This is an excellent month for expanding your social circle and meeting new people, so the key to love is making new friends by extending your social circle, traveling with colleagues, going to conferences, or joining social and political organizations.

Right now love begins with friendship, and the best way to establish a promising new romance is to find someone with whom you share passions and interests, that's why joining organizations that might involve a hobby or political interest is important.

If you are already in a romance, it's important that you guys begin to make friends with each other's friends, the more you and a partner have mutual friends, the more relationships are strengthened. Relationships where you have very different interests and different friendship groups are weakened this month.

Aquarius looking for love, will find they are involved in relationships that are incredibly captivating, mystical and emotional right now, however although these relationships often get off to a very quick start, they can later become incredibly complicated. So while there's a lot of excitement and anticipation in love right now, it's important to be aware that there could be a long and winding road that you are about to embark on.

Career and Aspiration

This month Mars enters Scorpio which signals a very busy and exciting phase in your career, and it's very important for you to be assertive and courageous.

This is an excellent phase for Aquarius who are self-employed and work of their own initiative, as you enjoy motivating yourself, exploring interesting goals and setting yourself challenges.

This is a much more difficult month for Aquarius who work under supervision and it may be a time for you to acknowledge that you need more freedom within your career to truly expand, and this can be the impetus for a new career. If you decide on a new career, this is a fantastic time for looking for jobs, sending out résumés or doing an intensive training course to prepare for a new role.

You should seek out leadership roles, and even if you are employment you should take the lead on moral and ethical issues.

You should be using your unique skills to be ingenious, inventive and forward-thinking, to make an impression on other people and to generate a lot of self-confidence in your unique Aquarius talents.

As an Aquarius, you can often feel like a square peg in a round hole simply because you have a rather eccentric and unusual nature, but your feeling of often being an outsider or not fitting in, is actually a great advantage, so play to it.

Adventure and Motivation

While you should be careful of dabbling in the occult, this is a month where you gain a lot of interesting experiences and enjoyment from alternative fields. You may find it interesting reading or studying esoteric subjects, holistic healing and subjects like hypnotism and dream analysis.

It is very helpful and enlightening for you to open your mind to different avenues of thought, and that's why you are prone to everything that it is a little bit subversive, mysterious and unknown.

You have a great taste for mystery this month and you can explore that in many different ways, including fiction writing and writing short stories, particularly if these require some research.

This is an excellent time to focus on the spiritual or the philosophical side of life. It's very important to have an understanding of what your mission in life is, and this is a chance to work on your own personal development by understanding what makes you tick as a person. Is it working with people? Is it having security? Is it gaining greater understanding? Or is it communication? As an Aquarius you are likely to be more inspired by activities that involve interaction with other people, gaining knowledge and improving understanding, you also tend to be inspired when you go places that no other people dare go. There's a part of your personality that is controversial, rebellious and is always looking to break new ground, so your focus this month should be doing something that no one else is doing or trying to understand something or articulate something that other people have a problem with.

Marriage and Family

This month is an important yet complicated one for long term relationships, as I mentioned in the opening sections, Pluto is about to move out of Capricorn and into Aquarius and this will be very significant for Aquarius, however this does mean that there are certain psychological aspects of yourself that are deeply buried, which you still need to confront before you can truly move forward.

These hidden aspects may come to light within your interaction with you partner. Often people try to hide aspects of themselves from themselves and from others, particularly regarding any base instincts that they feel are not suitable for polite society, but when these become suppressed, they operate in subversive ways because they undermine your conscious interactions.

This month anything which is not properly dealt with or acknowledged within yourself can cause disruption in relationships. In many cases a partner may act out these emotions, so if you look at you partner as a mirror to yourself it's often a clue to things that you need to be dealing with, and the sooner it's done the better and you own self development and improvement in relationships can take place.

Money and Finance

This month it's very important for you to listen to what's being said on the grapevine, friends may have useful advice for you about business or job prospects in general. The more social you are, the more you will get helpful leads and tips which can help you make money or make good decisions in business.

This may be a good time to travel with others to trade fairs, professional networking events and conferences. Information is key to success and you can get that information through conversation with others and the media.

No man is an island and this month the best way for you to proceed in your career is by paying attention to what's happening in society in terms of politics and new legislation.

Living and Loving to the Full

As adults we tend to self-censor, we often encourage ourselves to be mature and realistic, but along the way our hopes dreams and things which truly makes us happy can be forgotten about or sidelined, and somehow we become jaded and our zest for life can deteriorate.

However, what Aquarius can do this month to enhance love and magic is begin thinking again about the things that most excite and bring joy to your life. It's time to dust off you hopes and dreams that are long forgotten and for you and you partner to start re-engaging with life in a more positive, optimistic fashion where you both put yourselves first and do things that you truly enjoy.

So you and you partner should both encourage each other to take up new hobbies, make new friends or do new activities that will excite you guys and be very rewarding psychologically. It's important for you both to reestablish a strong bond of friendship and camaraderie and this can mean supporting and encouraging each other.

Planetary Cautions

This is often a month where they are strange coincidences and where things tend to come full circle, you may be more aware of the role fate and karma play in your life, but it's important for you not to be fatalistic, you must avoid thinking that anything is a fait accompli because you still have the power to change situations through being positive and proactive, and therefore you should not be defeatist.

It's very important for you to acknowledge any anger and resentment, and not to project these. Often right now your biggest enemy is yourself, so you must avoid seeing challenges in terms of other people or situations and rather see these challenges as a reflection of things within yourself that need to be adjusted, changed or grown out of.

Moon Magic

The new moon phase extends from the 14th of October to the 28th of October this waxing phase is the perfect fortnight for new initiatives, setting plans, establishing goals, starting anything prospective and being proactive. This is the action phase, details below:

In the waxing phase leadership, innovation, enterprise and new activities are favored. Good for artistic inspiration, performance and activities that require confidence. Suitable for competitive activities. A good time for physical therapy like osteotherapy, physiotherapy or occupational therapy. New technology to improve health is helpful.

You should be cautious in delegating, employing people, or starting a new job. Getting a pet or activities with pets is not favored. This is not a good waxing period for fad diets.
You need to be careful of mixing medications. You should be careful in striking or union activism.

NOVEMBER

Essence and Energies – "Pocket full of dreams."

This month the energies are very ambitious, but not always harmonious, as when you want something you want it desperately and you're extremely determined and can be quite assertive in getting what you need.

This is an excellent time for tackling anything that needs a lot of guts and determination, and it's also a good time for any physical activity that needs endurance and grit. You have a lot of mental and physical staying power right now, and you are ideally suited to tasks that need quite a lot of courage and audacity.

This month if you want anything badly enough you will crawl over broken glass to get it, and that's why you are often successful l. However, sometimes it's still important to acknowledge your own limits and the extent to which you may be burning bridges, because while the power is yours this month, you may unwittingly set certain karma into to play that you might have to deal with later.

Affirmation: "I resolve to use my power wisely."

Love and Romance

In terms of new relationships, humor and an open mind are really important, this is not a month to get incredibly intense or to take yourselves too seriously in a relationship. Where you are becoming too dogmatic or taking offence too easily, things can really struggle to be harmonious.

This can be a time of one night stands and hot and passionate love affairs with lots of chaotic excitement. You are drawn to people who have a very charismatic energy, this month the butterflies are going and an exotic new person may have come into your life. Right now you may feel quite intoxicated by love, so it's quite easy to get carried away with yourself and to be in love with love. There's nothing wrong with that however, because often a powerful love affair can unleash creative potential and be quite transformative for you.

So this is a month when you may take many risks in love, many of the things or people you are attracted to may be seen by others as bad for you. You can be reckless and a little bit risky in love but somehow you are drawn magnetically to people who are actually going to shake you up and show you something new about the world and yourself. You are sexually excited when you are shocked, so it's a time of being shaken and stirred.

It's ideal in a new relationship to be socializing and going out a lot, often communication can get in the way of a relationship really getting off to a good start, somehow the wrong things seem to get said, so it's much better if you can both focus your attention on exciting activities while providing each other with company rather than dominating each other's time and space by being in quiet intimate areas with a lot of pressure or where emotional intelligence is required.

Aquarius is quite tense this month and you can be quite snappy and that's why you need to have a lot of stimulation around you, rather than having to use you emotional intelligence in intimate situations because that can make you quite awkward.

Career and Aspiration

This is a time when you are very ambitious, you will put a lot of effort into furthering you career goals and sometimes this leads you into conflict situations. You may find that you are banging your head against a brick wall when it comes to people in authority, and everything takes that much longer simply because you tend to be in a situation where other people, who are more conservative or lazy, are dragging their feet.

It's very important for you to have more patience in terms of career, things can only go as fast as they can go and sometimes you don't acknowledge that everything has a natural tempo and flow.

You have to be more cognizant of using timing wisely, often you're a little bit hot headed and gung ho, and you fail to take account of entrenched viewpoints or sensitivities.

Adventure and Motivation

This is a fantastic month for Aquarius guys who are involved in any job or hobby where you have to present, educate or teach people. You love to lead the way and show how it's done, and you're inspired by any situation where you can demonstrate you skills or showcase you talents.

This is a time where you want to shine, you want to be appreciated and acknowledged and you gravitate to any situation where you can take the limelight. You don't want the limelight for the limelight's sake necessarily, but you do want to help educate and inspire others, and you really enjoy it when you get positive feedback and know that you've made a difference.

The focus this month is also breaking down barriers, it's important for you to identify the practical things, but also the people and attitudes that form a prison. We all tend to make our own prison, as we can be victims of our own consciousness. So this month it is time to understand that you are involuntarily bound by certain norms or parameters which you accept automatically and you should challenge those.

You should ask yourself where you are feeling stuck or restricted in your life, and then it's time for you to take action and that action should be holistic: it should be tackling any fears or anxieties about breaking those barriers; it should also be about rejecting societal norms that you don't feel should apply; and then it should be about taking practical steps with courage.

Marriage and Family

This is an ideal time for you and you partner to discuss long-term goals and to recommit to your future as a couple. It's time for you both to take a step back and see the bigger picture, it's very important that you don't become bogged down in minutiae or bickering.

It's also a time in relationships where it may be good for you both to take a spontaneous trip away for a weekend, or even a week if you can afford it. It's really important to bring a little bit of novelty and spontaneity into the relationship, don't forget that none of us can survive without fun and excitement and therefore this is a good month for you to surprise each other and to have conversations about adult things, rather than just having to discuss work, chores and family, and to start re-engaging with each other as two to individualistic people, rather than just doing mundane things as a couple.

Excellent time for date nights.

Money and Finance

A good month for financial decisions, making investments and organizing your finances, things should be ticking along quite nicely and you cash flow should be improving.

You should feel more confident about making business and

management decisions, and it's generally easier to organize you financial affairs and get on top of paperwork.

This is a good time for reviewing assets and maybe purchasing new equipment to increase efficiency, it may also be a time when you spend more money on enhancing you reputation with a better website, signage on you premises or rewriting you CV and updating professional profiles.

Living and Loving to the Full

This month enhancing love magic is all about the level of positivity in the relationship and also faith. Every relationship needs a vision and often relationships go downhill when both partners stop believing in each other, stop believing in love or stop believing that the relationship has the potential to grow and become rewarding once again.

All relationships go through periods of difficulty or at the very least a doldrums, where not a lot is happening and where you can both feel bored or uninspired by each other. That's why it's always important to recognize where a relationship is and to adjust your approach so the relationship stays fresh and doesn't become jaded. So enhancing love magic this month it's all about reinvigorating an enthusiasm or belief in the potential of relationship.

Planetary Cautions

The key phrase for this month is 'too much of a good thing', you really have to be careful not to go overboard, your enthusiasm and desires tend to get the better of you and your self-control is tested.

You're often quite strung up and you can be dealing with a lot of pressures at work and at home, and things can reach fever pitch. It's very important for you to look after your health and your heart health, you should eat sensibly and avoid too many stimulants or alcohol.

The key this month is everything in moderation, and you need to take a step back and understand when you're may be throwing the kitchen sink at something when a subtle approach would be better.

Moon Magic

The new moon phase extends from the 13th of November to the 27th of November this waxing phase is the perfect fortnight for new initiatives, setting plans, establishing goals, starting anything prospective and being proactive. This is the action phase, details below:

The waxing phase is not great for strenuous physical exercise or work. This is not a good time for risky ventures and doing things suddenly in which you have little experience. Competitive events, debate and aggressive activities are not favored. Not a great time for radical image changes.

This is not a suitable time for a new job or role at work. This is not a suitable waxing phase for new diets, joining a gym or a radical change in diet. Balance and moderation is needed in health and you should be more concerned about health matters, although you should do thorough research before deciding on a path.

Recruitment and outsourcing is not favored. New business in the service sector is not favored. Better and deeper understanding is needed of health issues, root causes and nutrition.

This period favors dealing decisively with financial matters. You may get more responsibility organizing and investing funds for others. An important time to improve sex life or address problems in sex life. Research and development and also renovation is successful. It's an excellent time for new business in investment management and accounting or audit.

Energies and Essence – "Oh, what a night.
Late December back in '23.
What a very special time for me,
'Cause I remember what a night."

December has much to offer you, and you will feel less inhibited and like a free spirit set loose in a new universe. You are naturally are spontaneous, and you will encounter many new groups of people with ideas that can excite you, stimulate you, or rouse you to act in some way. Interaction with other people is no longer just about a tick box social life of predictable and dull outings with people you long since lost connection with. This is about connecting with people who are part of your future not your past, people who have pearls of wisdom to bring into your life. They say when the pupil is ready, the teacher will emerge, and this year there will be many 'teachers' emerging to help you on the stairway to new goals, often goals which were previously unimagined, but which suddenly take off quite spectacularly. Your connections with others are often erratic and subject to great flux, and at times it can be hard to keep up – it is often more about various lives touching and the interchange of energy rather than a time of series bonds forming. Take what you can from each encounter and never try and control events, let them lead you. Do not form expectations, and look for ways to shape events into those expectations; allow yourself freedom to explore and remold yourself by new realities.

Affirmation – "Multi new associations at the key to my future and welcome weird and wonderful experiences without prejudice."

Love and Romance

This is an excitable and inspired month when it comes to dating and you're likely to pursue new love interests or take the first steps to initiate a relationship. However things are likely to go slightly awry, you must listen to your instincts and follow you gut, but you should also apply emotional intelligence because it's easy for you to put your foot in it and make the wrong moves.

While you can certainly make a good start and get your foot in the door with a new romantic partner, things with this person may be far more complex that you first realize and a relationship may take a lot more time and effort than you anticipate. You're probably looking for fun and light-hearted romance, but you're going to get something a little bit more taxing.

This doesn't mean however a relationship that begins now doesn't have potential, it's just that it's not quite what you think it's going to be, it's a little be a little more of a rollercoaster.

Career and Aspiration

This is a really good month for celebrating with colleagues and you may receive a promotion or recognition. You may have the opportunity to attend an awards ceremony or get some sort of acknowledgement.

This can be quite a fun time within the work sphere, you may be more involved in promotions, advertising and the seasonal activities to do with your business, or it may be the case that everyone office is in a really good mood and this helps to make the month go swimmingly.

This is an ideal time for enhancing you image and reputation, so anything you do within you social media profile or in terms of public engagements or speeches you give can help you to impress both your boss colleagues and the public.

You tend to be in demand, you're appreciated and people want more of your ideas or you artistic input.

Adventure and Motivation

This month Aquarius thrives on spontaneity, nervous energy and a sense of fun. You can be mischievous and may rock the boat with provocative behavior.

You enjoy expressing your views and brainstorming with others, the cogs in your head are always turning. You're into information and can be obsessive about looking for data.

December is an ideal time to execute an idea that you have had in the back of your mind for a while, but it should be something you're quite passionate about. You're not competitive as such as you're eager to share any breakthroughs or progress with others.

It is time when you're really talkative and expressive and so it's excellent for a social media campaigns, starting blogs or vlogs or being more visible online as well as in real life.

This time is ripe for communication and sharing of ideas, and it brings you a great deal of stimulation, even if it's not immediately constructive.

Marriage and Family

In existing relationships and marriages, you may stir things up quite unconsciously in order to take things to a new level by disrupting the equilibrium. You may be accused by you partner of looking for arguments, but you are really eager to get deeper conversation going. You need to find constructive ways of engaging with you partner about deeper and more sensitive subjects – you shouldn't be argumentative or create tension in order to get around to saying what is on you mind: perhaps reading books or seeing movies that are about the topic you want to talk about can be used as a springboard.

This can be a very interesting holiday season, especially if you partner shares the same desire for renewed intimacy and escapism as you – use your combined creativity to create magic moments and memories. Sometimes Aquarians provoke passion in others as they are not able to easily access that passion themselves; this December you should use visualization to feel that passion and excitement within yourself and you should let go of the fear of losing your detachment.

Money and Finance

This month it is very much trying to see the wood for the trees and not becoming so bogged down in detail that you lose sight of the bigger picture and the end goal. You need to trust your intuition, and you also need to have a measure of faith (be it faith in the universe, God or yourself) that you will make the right money moves at the right time as it is just impossible to decide on logic and facts only.

You may just have to go with something that doesn't really make sense but which feels right. This is also a time where the more you look at something or research something, the more complicated it seems to get – perhaps you can only grasp it on an intuitive level. You also have to learn when to switch off and move on from things that are frustrating you.

Living and Loving to the Full

There is a need to break the unwritten rules of relationships right now and stir it up – you feel restless and will encourage you partner to try new things. You guys may spend some time apart with your respective friends, which can be a very good thing – all relationships need some space as too much routine and familiarity kill the mystery. If you and you partner go your separate ways on the weekend, you will miss each other. We all take people for granted at times, and some planned time apart is very beneficial. When you guys are together, you must refocus on foreplay and fantasy, lovemaking may have become too straightforward and too clockwork, you must get the feeling and the curiosity back into the mix – you must add an element of surprise to you sex life.

Planetary Cautions

Mercury is retrograde in you 12th house until the 13th, this affects your subconscious mind. You may have great difficulty making decisions, you could be plagued by self-doubt. Like the previous retrograde in May, this one also inclines you to be secretive, evasive and in search of solitude. You have a need for introspection during these periods and you're very good at procrastination and avoidance during these too.

You may be tired and you need rest and lots of water as you are probably run down and need a little battery recharge.

During this phase you may be prone to anxiety, you tend to worry and your imagination can play tricks on you . You should certainly avoid alcohol and toxic personality types as this feeds into depression or in general, the blues.

This is a phase where you need to keep you paint dry and just feel things out. It's not possible to see the whole picture clearly and thus some indecision is quite forgivable.

You're very impressionable during this phase and quite open to new ways of looking at life and so have some heart to hearts. You will open up sooner or later.

Moon Magic

The new moon phase extends from the 21th of January to the 5th of February, this waxing phase is the perfect fortnight for new initiatives, setting plans, establishing goals, starting anything prospective and being proactive. This is the action phase, details below:

Mercury goes direct on 19th in Capricorn indicating that you're less anxious and more settled in your thinking. This is a good time to analys, prepare and get your thoughts together. It's great for deep thinking, using positive visualization and affirmations. Creative activities especially to do with using imagination and becoming inspired are favored. A good time for spiritual awareness and going on retreats.

This is an excellent time for getting married or engaged. It's also a favorable waxing phase for changes and new starts in long term relationships. Negotiations and legal matters are successful. A good time to get advice or counselling. Careers involving law, mediation and consulting are favored.

This is not a good time for real estate deals or looking for property. Large family events and having people to stay is not favored. This is not a good time to open a new business in the hospitality, tourism or environment industry.

This is also not a favorable waxing phase for long haul travel, starting a new academic or higher education course or publishing. Advertising and promotional activities are not successful not is new import export business.

A good period for meditation and mindfulness. Pursuits like yoga, homeopathy and holistic health are successful. This favors new endeavors of a charitable nature. A good time to set up business connected to music, medicine, healing or the ocean.

Mars goes direct in Gemini on the 13th indicating momentum for creative and artistic ventures. Work with children and young people is successful. A good time for competitive activities and innovation. Dating and romantic pursuits and date nights can yield problems.

Well that's a wrap of my biggest most comprehensive Aquarius Horoscope yet.

Whether you are a Aquarius or know a Aquarius, I do believe you will have found this very helpful and informative.

I aim to give you a variety of advice based on psychology, spiritual insight, relationship advice and business guidance, so you get a little bit of everything.

Take care and have a wonderful 2023.

Blessings, Lisa.